Yarns for Textile Crafts

Tessa Lorant

VNR VAN NOSTRAND REINHOLD COMPANY

To the memory of Ralph R. Lorant

Copyright © 1984 by Tessa Lorant
Library of Congress Catalog Card Number 83-16945
ISBN 0-442-25978-6

Printed in the United States of America
Designed by Dudley Thomas

Published by Van Nostrand Reinhold Company Inc.
135 West 50th Street
New York, New York 10020

Van Nostrand Reinhold Company Limited
Molly Millars Lane
Wokingham, Berkshire RG11 2PY, England

Van Nostrand Reinhold
480 La Trobe Street
Melbourne, Victoria 3000, Australia

Macmillan of Canada
Division of Gage Publishing Limited
164 Commander Boulevard
Agincourt, Ontario M1S 3C7, Canada

16 15 14 13 12 11 10 9 8 7 6 5 4 3 2 1

Library of Congress Cataloging in Publication Data

Lorant, Tessa.
  Yarns for textile crafts.

  Bibliography: p. 152
  Includes index.
  1. Yarn. 2. Textile crafts. I. Title.
TT699.L67   1984   746'.028   83-16945
ISBN 0-442-25978-6

Contents

Tables

Acknowledgments

I would like to thank Friedie Peter for all her help in finding American suppliers of unusual and interesting yarns; Candace Bahouth for permission to photograph some of her work to illustrate the imaginative use of yarns in tapestry weaving (figures 2, 6-10, 8-2, and 8-3); Eileen Bird for providing hand-spinning materials to be photographed, and for providing examples of hand-spun yarns and handwoven fabrics (figures 8, 1-6, 3-8); Richard Warburg for taking photographs of wool and cotton fibers through an electron microscope; Colin Warburg for technical assistance; the Misses Grocock of Allestree, Derbyshire, who loaned the christening robe (figure 4-6); Mrs. M. Dixon who loaned her mother's christening robe (figure 6); and Miss M. Hanson, of Coventry, who loaned her mother's handmade lace (figure 8-1) to be photographed.

I would also like to thank all the yarn manufacturers and suppliers who sent me samples or sample cards of their yarns; the American Wool Council for their interest and for sending me information on the educational materials they supply; Mr. G. Hellier, of Batch Farm, Godney, Somerset, England, for permission to photograph his crossbred Jacob sheep and polled Dorset sheep; and the London Zoo for permission to photograph the "Mouflon" sheep (figure 3-2).

Introduction

Some of the inventions of the late eighteenth century, such as the spinning jenny, the spinning mule, and the steam engine, contributed to a revolution in the textile industry. They released both women and men from the tedious chores associated with spinning yarn, cloth making, or fabric production (figure 1).

Weaving as an industry began in Europe in the fourteenth century and soon became a factor in political events. Wool, the indigenous fiber, became such a desirable commodity that eventually the export of wool and woolen goods from England was severely restricted. The early North American colonists, for example, were forced to build their own woolen indus-

Fig. 1.
A portable spinning wheel, often called a "gossip" wheel.

1

try. At first, the new American industry needed the support of the courts to ensure that sufficient yarn was spun. The General Court of Massachusetts, for instance, found it necessary to require youths to spin and weave and to order each family to spin yarn. Each family was assessed for a number of spinners, and each spinner was required to produce one pound of yarn per week, for thirty weeks of the year. The penalty for spinning short of this was quite severe. People were also encouraged to weave or knit their own fabrics, and perhaps sew them as well.

With the introduction of industrial methods and machines, the textile industry really began to flourish in both America and Europe. The home-based spinners, weavers, and knitters, though loath to lose their jobs, were keen to give up tedious work. Today virtually *all* yarn is spun in the industrial yarn mills on some of the most sophisticated machinery used in industry. Where at one time yarns were made only of natural fibers, the modern fiber industry now has a vast range of man-made, as well as natural, fibers at its disposal. The range grows larger every year. These fibers are mixed and mingled in an ever-increasing range of blends combined with new methods of spinning. Both the domestic textile crafter and the industrial clothing manufacturer have an enormous choice of yarns.

However, released from tedious and repetitive work, people began to feel deprived of the satisfaction of producing beautiful textiles with their own hands. The satisfaction of creating a woven, knitted, or crocheted fabric, such as a tapestry weaving (figure 2) or a knitted lace (figure 3), with

[handwritten margin note: Not True even in 1984]

Fig. 2.
Tapestry weaving: George Washington.

Fig. 3.
Traditional, hand-knitted Viennese lace.

nothing more than a few simple tools, willing hands, and yarn, is once more becoming popular. People from all walks of life are rediscovering the very real pleasure to be gained by using their hands for all manner of crafts; the textile crafts are, perhaps, the most popular. They provide a source of fabrics that can be used to make beautiful clothes, fine furnishings, or artistic hangings.

The tools, for the most part, can be very simple; a crochet hook, a pair of knitting needles, a rug hook (figure 4), a simple loom, a lacemaker's pillow together with a few bobbins. The willing hands are only too eager to pass the work through their fingers, and there is also more leisure time to do it. The shorter working week—made possible by modern technology—has contributed to the availability of many more hours for recreation, and these hours are being used to an increasing extent for creative work in the textile crafts. Not only are such crafts satisfying to do, they are also a

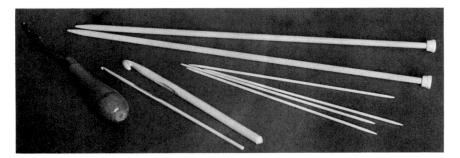

Fig. 4. *Rug hook, knitting needles, and crochet hook.*

relaxing way to combat the stresses of modern life. Many doctors now consider knitting as the ultimate stress therapy for both men and women. These crafts are for everyone, and they provide one of the most rewarding outlets for the creative urge. But there is one more ingredient needed for each and every textile craft, and that is the raw material—the yarn—without which no textile project can be created.

What many crafters often do not realize is that "knitting wool," or "weaving yarn," is not something that can simply be bought in a store or ordered by mail. *Which* yarn you use is all-important. The finest tools, the greatest talent, the most expensive and beautiful-looking yarn cannot usefully be turned into the fabric of your dreams unless *you* choose the yarn that will match the result you wish to achieve. And that choice is very large. It needs to be an informed one if your project is to be successful as well as enjoyable.

The wide choice of yarns brings a certain onus with it. Making that choice is as much a part of any craft as are the tools you use or the techniques you master. This book sets out to explain what yarn is, what it is made of, how it is put together, which type of yarn to use in your favorite textile craft, where to find the yarn, and how much you should pay for it. It tells how yarns are measured and how to estimate the amount of yarn you will need for a particular project; it explains the mill's yarn measurement system so

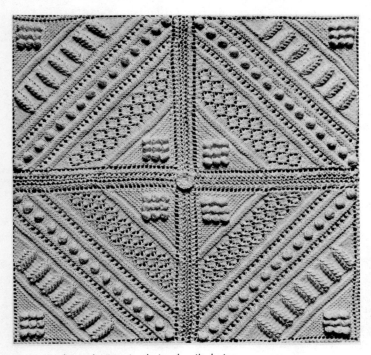

Fig. 5. *Traditional, Victorian knitted quilt design.*

you will not have to rely on the vague names given in most retail yarn stores. There is a section on how to reuse unraveled yarn and another one on how to combine commercially manufactured yarns to design your own individual yarn.

As textile crafters become more sophisticated about the qualities of different yarns, retailers will stock more of the kinds of yarns that will enable you to create exciting, versatile, and, above all, original and individual fabrics. Furthermore, "industrial" weaving and knitting yarns can make a big contribution to cutting the costs and increasing the combinations of yarns for domestic crafters.

Making fabric is what textile craft is all about. There is no need to imitate the often excellent products of the textile factories; there *is* a need to produce distinctive, individual work—fabric that you cannot buy for any amount of money, fabric that will enhance a wardrobe or home furnishings in a way that mass-produced materials, however beautiful, never can (figure 5). Making such a material may take many hours, but the textile crafter will gain great satisfaction from producing a fabric that can last not only for the lifetime of the person who has made it, but for many years

Fig. 6.
A hand-worked christening gown, over one hundred years old.

beyond. In this way the long hours that some textile projects can take to complete will be "time efficient." Choose the right yarns and your work can be shown with pride by your descendants, as much an heirloom as any work of the past—a testament to the creative urge in all of us and to the re-emergence of true craft after the predominance of the mass-produced articles of the last hundred years or more (figures 6, 7, and 8).

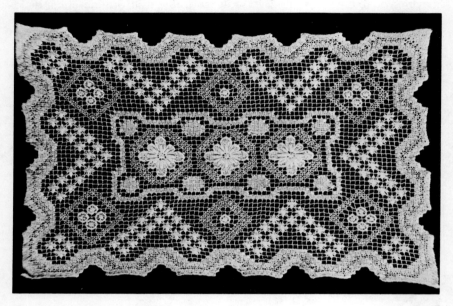

Fig. 7. *Traditional, hand-worked Cretan lace.*

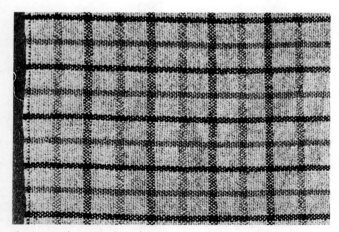

Fig. 8. *Handwoven worsted.*

1/ Definitions

Most people already know that the word *yarn* means a thread made by twisting fibers, such as cotton or wool, and that yarn is the raw material used for weaving, knitting, crochet, and other textile crafts. This is true as far as it goes, but in order to make real use of these raw materials one needs to be a little more specific.

The textile industry, like any other area of specialization, has its own special technical language—its jargon. This book is for the layperson. Technical terms are only used when essential, but many of the words used in the textile world have an ordinary, as well as a technical, meaning. Also, they often have more than one meaning in the technical sense, which can lead to confusion when discussing particular subjects. A brief glossary is given at the back of this book, but each term is also elaborated on in the text where it is the most relevant.

Before considering a more precise definition of yarn, we need to know something about the meaning of the phrase *textile fiber*. Some fibers are not textile fibers, but this book is only concerned with those fibers that can be used to make yarn. The primary characteristic of a textile fiber is that it is considerably longer than it is wide; that is, it has a very high length-to-breadth ratio (see table 1). Textile fibers also need to be fine, strong, and flexible enough to be spun into an indefinite length (figure 1-1).

The description *textile* used before the word *fiber* means that the fiber in question must have the capacity to be woven, felted, knitted, or otherwise manipulated to make a textile material. This book is concerned only with those processes that require a yarn; felting, for instance, is not relevant.

Textile fibers can be divided into two types—filaments and staples.

Table 1. Length : Breadth Ratios of Some Staple Fibers

Fiber Type	Average Length	Average Width	Length: Breadth Ratio
Cotton	1 in. (2.5 cm.)	.0007 in. (18 microns)	1400 : 1
Flax	1 in. (2.5 cm.)	.0008 in. (20 microns)	1200 : 1
Wool	3 in. (7.5 cm.)	.001 in. (25 microns)	3000 : 1
Cashmere	3 in. (7.5 cm.)	.0006 in. (15 microns)	5000 : 1
Sisal	.118 in. (.3 cm.)	.0009 in. (24 microns)	130 : 1

Fig. 1-1.
Shetland wool fibers.

Filaments

The word *filament* describes fibers that are already sufficiently long to make yarn without any further process being necessary. The only natural filament fiber is silk, which is spun by the silkworm. The double threads (baves) from one silkworm cocoon can be up to two miles long. Silk is a very fine fiber, and is not strong enough on its own to make a yarn for domestic textile crafts. Several baves have to be combined to make a reeled (wound from silk filaments) yarn (see chapter 4).

Man-made textile fibers are also initially produced in the form of filaments. Spinning solutions are forced through holes in a spinneret (a metallic cap or nozzle perforated with between one and many thousands of holes) and emerge as filaments into a coagulating medium such as water or air. The size of the holes determines the size of the filaments, so that monofilament (single filament) yarns of adequate strength can be made in this way. Monofilament yarns are primarily used in industry, but most people are familiar with transparent nylon sewing thread (figure 1-2). Generally, however, the filaments are made much finer and grouped together to make multifilament yarns that are much more pliable and flexible than monofilament yarns. The number of filaments grouped, and often twisted, together to form a viable yarn is in the range of fifteen to one hundred (figure 1-3).

Fig. 1-2. *Magnified monofilament nylon.*

Fig. 1-3.
Multifilament nylon used to make a 3-ply knitting yarn.

Staples

The word *staple* describes fibers of relatively short length, varying from fiber to fiber and within the fiber group itself. Wool fiber, for instance, has a staple length from 1 to 16 inches (2.5 to 40 cm.), depending on the breed and part of the sheep it comes from.

Staple yarns depend for their length on a usually specially prepared mass of fibers being put together, drafted (drawn out), and twisted. Generally, textile fibers more or less cling together without having to be twisted together, but the twisting does make the fibers intertwine in such a way that pulling along the length will not immediately break the yarn. By combining fibers together in this way, even quite short staples can be turned into continuous, useful, and very strong yarn. Cotton staple, for instance, ranges from only ½ to 2½ inches (1 to 6.5 cm.) in length, yet cotton buttonhole thread, for example, is so strong that it is hard to break; scissors are needed to cut it (figure 1-4).

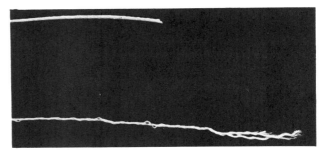

Fig. 1-4.
Top: cotton buttonhole thread needs scissors to cut it. Bottom: ordinary cotton sewing thread, torn, leaving a jagged edge.

A great deal of the yarn used for the domestic textile crafts is made from staples rather than filaments. This is true even of the man-made yarns that start out as filaments but are often turned into staples at a later stage. The extruded *tow* (the ropelike strand made up of all the filaments from a spinneret) is either cut into relatively small sections or processed in such a way that the filaments tear into staple lengths as the tow is being processed. The resulting staple lengths are then spun (see below) in ways similar to those used for other staple fibers.

Spinning

The word *spinning* is used in two technical senses. In the first sense, it means to turn a melt (spinning solution) into a filament by extruding it through a spinneret. In the case of silk the spinneret is a special gland in the silkworm that produces two filaments; in the case of man-made fibers the spinneret, as already mentioned, is a metallic cap with a predetermined number of small size holes that produces from one to thousands of filaments. The size and cross-sectional shape of these holes is also controlled, as discussed in chapter 6.

In the second sense, spinning means to draft (pull out) and twist prepared staple textile fibers. There are several ways of accomplishing this type of spinning, and the methods employed will depend on the type of textile fiber used and the desired end result (see chapter 6).

Singles Yarn

You are now in a position to understand a more precise definition of a strand of yarn. The strand is made from twisted or untwisted filament fibers or by twisting together prepared staple fibers held together by their clinging interaction. This strand is known as a "singles" or "single" yarn (s), whether it is twisted or untwisted, and whether it is made up of one filament (monofilament), several filaments (multifilament), or spun staples. The method of spinning and the amount of twist are important constituents of the yarn—just as important as the fibers used. More generally, then, you could say that a singles yarn consists of (twisted or untwisted) prepared fibers put together in such a way that they make a long, relatively thin, continuously available, flexible connection that does not immediately tear when force is applied along its length.

Some singles are used as they are, particularly in industry, but also for some domestic textile crafts. Shetland lace, for instance, is shown to advantage when knitted with the singles "cobweb" yarn available direct from Shetland or specialist suppliers (figure 1-5). Though coarse by comparison with the fine spinning done in Shetland at the turn of the century, when the gossamer yarn needed to make the "wedding-ring" shawls took as long to spin as it took to knit the shawl, this is the finest Shetland wool yarn now available. Tweed, too, is woven from singles yarns (figure 1-6). These singles were originally called cheviots. Many hand-knitted ethnic garments are worked in bulky singles, such as the Icelandic Lopis (figure 1-7).

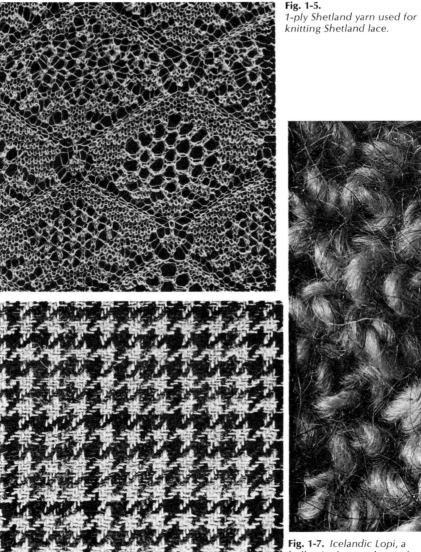

Fig. 1-5.
1-ply Shetland yarn used for knitting Shetland lace.

Fig. 1-7. *Icelandic Lopi, a bulky singles, used to make a looped, knitted fabric.*

Fig. 1-6. *Handwoven tweed made with singles.*

Folded Yarns

The great majority of yarns, however, are folded: two or more singles are put together in some way to increase the strength and generally the evenness of the yarn. There are various methods of folding and these are discussed in chapter 6. But the term *yarn* can mean a singles strand or a folding of any number of strands, though the number does not normally exceed six (figure 1-8). Knitters are used to speaking in terms of 2-ply, 3-ply, and 4-ply yarns to show the thickness of the yarn they are using; but plying simply means folding. As explained in chapter 7, this is not a reliable way to measure the thickness of yarns, even of knitting fingerings (yarns specially spun for hand-knitting), as the thickness of the original singles will vary from mill to mill and from grade to grade of fiber. What is important to stress at this point is that yarns may be made of a combination of singles, and that the combination can be as diverse as the initial processes used to make the singles yarn. Novel ways of folding create the "novelty" or "fancy" yarns (figure 1-9). Details are given in chapter 6.

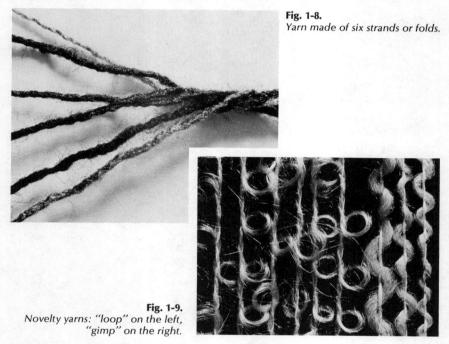

Fig. 1-8.
Yarn made of six strands or folds.

Fig. 1-9.
Novelty yarns: "loop" on the left, "gimp" on the right.

Cabled or Corded Yarns

Two or more folded yarns can also be combined by twisting them together (figures 1-10 and 1-11). These yarns are not as popular for knitting as they are for some other textile crafts; however, most crochet yarns, sewing threads, crêpe yarns, and so on are examples of cabled or corded yarns.

Combination Yarns

Filament and spun staple yarns can be combined to give strength to yarn made from a relatively weak staple fiber, say, or to add something of the unique properties of a natural fiber to a synthetic one.

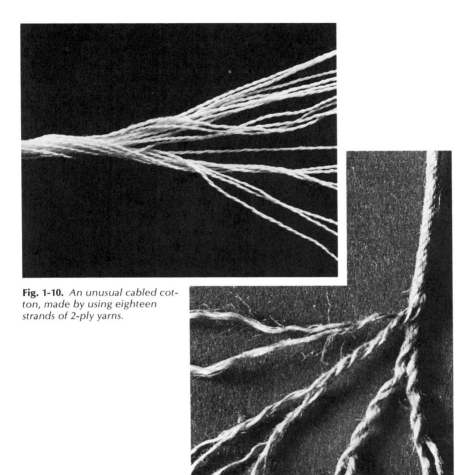

Fig. 1-10. *An unusual cabled cotton, made by using eighteen strands of 2-ply yarns.*

Fig. 1-11. *A cabled linen, made by combining three strands of 6-ply yarn.*

Textured Yarns

Many yarns made from long-stapled fibers are given warmth, bulk, and interest by "brushing," that is, deliberately disentangling some of the fibers from the smooth yarn structure and making them stand out at an angle to the length (figure 1-12). Brushing is particularly popular for mohair or mohair-type knitting yarns, as the mohair fiber is strong and long enough to withstand this treatment without being pulled out of the yarn structure.

Many man-made filament yarns can be processed to produce distortions along the filament lengths, such as crimps, loops, and coils. The filaments will no longer lie parallel to one another, and this can add desirable characteristics as well as interesting looks to yarns made from them (see figure 1-3).

Fig. 1-12. *"Brushed" yarns used for a "tabby" weave. The yarn structure almost hides the structure of the fabric.*

Blended Yarns

Several types of fiber can be blended together so that mixtures of natural and man-made fiber yarns can be spun. Such yarns will combine properties from each of the fibers in the single yarn, though the properties themselves will not always be in direct proportion to the blend. A blended yarn made of equal parts of cotton and nylon will not be as strong as a pure nylon yarn because the nylon is elastic and the cotton inelastic. Consequently, when the yarn is stretched the cotton fibers will snap and weaken the yarn.

Prefabricated Yarns

We can still add to the description of yarn. A viable raw material for textile crafts can be made from previously manufactured fabric. A good example is "chenille yarn," which can be produced by first weaving small groups of warp yarns in a cross-weave, then cutting between these groups to form strips of yarn (figure 1-13). Braids (three or more threads interlaced by plaiting) can be used for unusual effects, especially if made of metallic yarns (figure 1-14). Rag rugs are yet another example of how "yarn" can be produced from previously woven or knitted fabric.

Narrow ribbon is becoming very popular for use as a material for knitting and weaving in the same way as spun yarns, though ribbon may well require more skill and experience to use it satisfactorily. Some manufacturers now market ribbons made specially for textile crafting (figures 1-15 and 1-16).

Fig. 1-13. *"Chenille" yarn.*

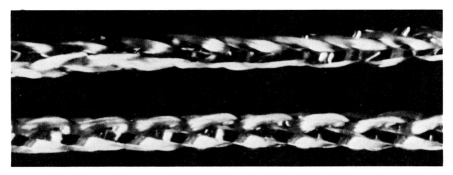

Fig. 1-14. *Braided metallic yarn.*

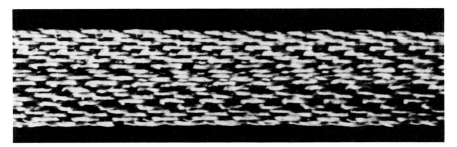

Fig. 1-15. *Woven rayon ribbon.*

Fig. 1-16. *Woven silk ribbon and "fancy" ribbon.*

Definition of Yarn

By now you should have some idea of what a definition of yarn might be, and what it would imply: Yarn is a structure of substantial length, with a relatively small cross section, but of reasonable tensile strength, consisting of filament and/or staple textile fibers that may have had a texturing process applied to them, or consisting of strips of previously formed material, twisted or untwisted, along the length.

This definition will include the finest sewing thread and the coarsest chenille yarn, the sheerest metallic strip and the crudest nylon monofilament. It will imply a huge range of yarns because the mixture of different fibers, colors, fiber blends, methods of spinning, folding, cabling, and texturing, as well as methods of preparing strips from previously produced material, can all be intermingled to give an enormous variety.

Not all yarns will be equally suitable for all textile crafts, however well the yarns may have been made in the first place. Yarn quality is therefore dependent on the end use of the yarn. This is discussed in chapter 9.

2/ Textile Fiber Properties and Characteristics

No single textile fiber will ever have all the properties you might consider desirable in such a fiber. Some properties are useful for one purpose, some for another, and the two may not be compatible. Both wool and flax are excellent textile fibers, but a linen fabric will be much more comfortable in hot weather than even the highest quality worsted made from the finest wool. The choice of textile fiber and the way it is processed will produce the yarn most suited to the particular project you have in mind.

Processing the fiber into yarn can alter its primary characteristics considerably, and the method of making a fabric will influence the results still further. Nevertheless, certain characteristics will be inherent in the fiber, and these can only be modified. The main properties of particular fibers are listed in table 2 for easy reference and are further discussed in chapters 3 through 5.

Comfort

Where the ultimate aim of the textile craft is to produce apparel, the relationship between fiber properties and the comfort of the wearer of the fabric made of such fibers is of primary importance.

Absorbency and Moisture Retention

Fibers vary considerably in their capacity to absorb moisture. Good moisture absorption, an important property, means that perspiration can readily be taken up. Generally, the natural fibers such as wool, cotton, and silk have good absorption rates. Many of the synthetic fibers absorb very little water, so that fabrics made of them are uncomfortable to wear in humid conditions and can feel clammy in any weather. Filament synthetic fibers show poor absorption more than staple fibers of the same type.

Elasticity

Some fibers, when stretched, will spring back to their normal length much more readily than others. Wool, for instance, is one of the most elastic natural fibers, and nylon is one of the most elastic synthetic fibers (figure 2-1). Both the methods of yarn construction and of fabric construction will affect the amount of elasticity in a garment, but whatever the processes used to produce it, the greater the elasticity of the fiber, the more comfortable the fabric will be to wear.

Table 2. Main Fiber Properties and Characteristics

	Acetate	Acrylic	Alpaca and Llama	Angora	Cashmere	Cotton	Linen	Metallic	Mohair	Nylon	Polyester	Rayon	Silk	Wool (Woolen-Spun)	Wool (Worsted-Spun)
Absorbency	-	O	X	X	X	X	X	O	X	-	O	X	X	X	X
Bleaching	-	X	O	O	O	X	X	O	O	X	X	-	-	X	X
Drapability	-	-	X	-	X	O	-	O	X	-	-	X	X	X	X
Durability	-	X	X	X	X	-	X	X	X	X	X	-	X	X	X
Elasticity	-	O	X	X	X	O	O	O	X	X	O	-	X	X	X
Heat Conductivity	-	O	O	O	O	-	X	X	O	O	-	X	O	O	O
Luster	X	X	X	-	O	-	X	X	X	X	-	X	X	O	-
Pilling	X	X	X	X	X	O	O	O	O	X	X	-	O	X	-
Quick Drying	-	X	O	O	O	O	O	-	O	-	-	O	-	O	O
Resilience	-	X	X	-	X	O	O	O	X	X	X	O	X	X	X
Resistance to:															
Abrasion	O	O	-	-	O	-	X	-	-	X	X	O	-	-	X
Light	-	X	-	-	-	O	-	-	-	-	X	O	O	O	-
Moths	X	X	-	-	-	X	X	X	-	X	X	X	X	O	O
Mildew	-	X	O	O	O	O	O	X	O	X	X	O	O	O	O
Shrinkage	X	O	X	X	X	X	X	O	-	O	O	X	X	X	X
Softness	-	X	-	X	X	O	O	O	-	-	-	-	X	X	X
Strength:															
Wet	O	O	O	O	O	X	X	-	-	X	X	O	O	O	O
Dry	-	-	-	-	O	X	X	-	-	X	X	-	-	O	-
Warmth	-	X	X	X	X	O	O	O	X	-	-	-	X	X	X

This table gives *indications* of the fiber characteristics.
X = characteristic of the fiber
- = characteristic of some of the fibers in this group
O = not characteristic of this fiber

Thermal Properties

Fibers are not in themselves either hot or cold; they take on the ambient temperature of their surroundings.

Heat Conductivity The rate at which body temperature is lost depends on whether the body covering will "conduct" heat away from the body. A "bad" conductor of heat will not disperse body temperature; heat can build up inside the body covering, and the wearer will feel warm. There is a

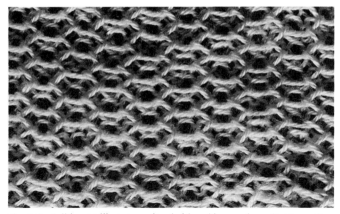

Fig. 2-2. A "thermal" yarn made of chlorofiber and acrylic fiber; the fabric construction also helps to conserve warmth.

Fig. 2-1.
A small length of nylon yarn can be stretched appreciably, showing the yarn's elasticity.

simple test for determining whether a fabric made from a particular fiber is a good or a bad conductor of heat: wrap a section of the fabric around a finger. Your finger will feel warm if the fabric is made of a fiber which is a bad conductor of heat. Several synthetic fibers feel warm in this sense; they include the acrylics, in particular chlorofiber, which is often used to make "thermal" underwear (figure 2-2).

Lofty Fibers Air spaces are excellent conservers of temperature. Some fibers trap tiny air pockets in their structure and are said to be "lofty." Fabrics made of such fibers will be warm to wear.

Wool fibers are good examples of lofty fibers. Wool fibers have scales on their outer covering (figure 2-3). These scales ensure that there will be pockets of air when the fibers are pressed against each other in the yarn structure. Furthermore, the large amount of crimp (waviness) in many wool fibers will also ensure that air pockets will be trapped in the yarn made of them. Wools vary in the number of scales per unit length and in the amount of crimp they possess. The finer wools have more scales and crimp and so will be the warmer ones (figure 1-1).

Though synthetic fibers start out as smooth filaments, they can be processed so that their texture resembles the crimp of wool.

Wet Heat Yet another property affects the warmth potential of a fiber. Some fibers give out heat when they are wet. This is particularly true of wool and to a much smaller extent of viscose rayon and cotton. Nylon and

Fig. 2-3. *A high magnification of wool fiber shows the scales on the fiber surface. (Photo: Richard Warburg)*

Fig. 2-4.
A lock of Wensleydale wool, showing a fair amount of crimp for a long-stapled wool.

other synthetics do not have this property in any great amount and that is why wool is still unsurpassed for warmth in cold, damp climates. Wool also protects against chilling after physical exertion, and this explains the use of the word *sweater* to mean a garment worn after exercise to prevent chilling. Originally sweaters were made of wool.

Looks

Making good-looking fabrics is probably the primary aim of domestic textile crafters. Several important properties contribute to the look of a fabric.

Drapability

The springiness, that is, the resilience, of the fiber will contribute substantially to the drapability of a fabric. Apart from that, the "weight," or relative density, of the fiber used, thickness for thickness, is an important aspect affecting the way the eventual fabric will hang and fall. Some rayons, for instance, give a certain weight that wools do not have. Static electricity, too, can affect the drapability of the fabric.

Affinity to Dyes

Fibers vary in the way they can absorb dyes; some are more porous than others and easily take up and retain dyes. Many fibers can be dyed through simple home methods, while others are very hard to dye, requiring complicated dyestuffs and procedures which may depend on special machinery. Industrial dyeing methods and materials have improved considerably recently, but deep colors may be expensive to prepare and some fibers are only offered in pastel shades.

Reaction to Bleaches

It may be necessary to bleach fibers before color can be added. Bleaching is not necessary for the man-made fibers that can now be manufactured in whatever pale shade is required. However, some natural fibers, such as alpaca or wild silk, may be relatively dark-colored in the raw state. Some of these fibers can be hard to bleach light enough to take pastel dye shades. This type of fiber is, therefore, often marketed in its "natural" color, not necessarily as it came from the fleece or the cocoon, but after blending with several fiber colors to give a uniform shade (figure 2-5).

Many light-colored natural fibers can be dyed at home as they are. Others can be prepared by bleaching with hydrogen peroxide or chlorine.

Luster

The amount of sheen in a fiber depends on the way light is reflected from the fiber surfaces. Though the finishing will affect the amount of luster, the fiber itself is very important. This explains why wool that has been dyed to exactly the same shade as a synthetic yarn might look quite different: the wool will have a mat look, the synthetic a shiny one (figure 2-6). The greater the number of reflecting surfaces, dispersing light rather than reflecting it

Fig. 2-5. *Four shades of cashmere fiber.*

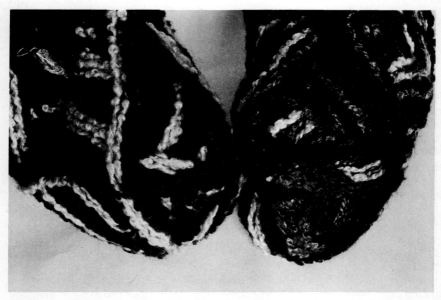

Fig. 2-6. *A random-dyed wool bouclé yarn on the left, the same random-dyed color in an acrylic on the right. The acrylic has more luster.*

in one direction, the more the end product will have a mat look, so fine fibers will produce a less shiny yarn than coarse fibers of the same type. Filament yarns will be much shinier than staple yarns made of the same fiber, and crimped or high-bulk synthetic yarns will be much less shiny than their untextured counterparts.

Resilience
The way a fiber reacts to being crushed or compressed is very important. The greater its ability to spring back to its original size after heat or weight has been applied, the better it will look. Clothes will shed creases easily and will not wrinkle. The high resilience of both wool and nylon, for instance, makes these attractive fibers, suitable for use in carpets. The greater abrasion resistance of nylon makes it a better choice for areas that receive heavy wear.

Static Electricity
When fibers are rubbed against each other, causing friction, a type of energy called "static electricity" will be generated. All fibers will store "static" in a dry atmosphere, but the electricity will leak away when there is any moisture present. Consequently, fibers that have low moisture absorption tend to generate a good deal of static under ordinary conditions, because they will be relatively dry. Garments made of such fibers may cling inelegantly to the body, and may crackle or spark when the garment is taken off. They will attract both dust and dirt.

Static is a much greater problem with synthetic than with natural fibers, which, as discussed above, are much greater absorbers of moisture.

Thermoplasticity
Many fibers, and the yarns made of them, are thermoplastic. A thermoplastic fiber or yarn can be manipulated into a crimped, coiled, looped, or other shape while being processed, and then subjected to a predetermined amount of heat for a specific period of time. Provided the level of heat is not exceeded after this "heat-setting" treatment, such yarn can be laundered, dry-cleaned, stretched, and compressed without distorting it in any way.

Maintenance and Care
Whether or not a fabric can easily be laundered depends not only on the particular fiber and its characteristics, but also on the way the fiber or yarn has been processed. Yarns manufactured to be used for industrial weaving or knitting are now sold to domestic crafters, often as "mill ends." However, unless the retailer selling the yarn has some idea of the end use for which the yarn was originally intended, difficulties can arise.

Stability
Yarn stability may depend on the process used in yarn preparation as well as on fiber characteristics. Sometimes yarns are deliberately made unstable

to achieve a particular purpose after fabric construction. Figure 2-7 shows an ordinary-looking cone (yarn wound on a conical support) of industrial singles nylon. The general assumption that nylon does not shrink is very misleading in this case. Figure 2-8 shows a strand of this yarn as it is when unwound from the cone, as well as a strand of the same yarn after it has been stretched and then released. If this nylon is used straight from the cone for domestic machine-knitting, say, and the knitted fabric is then immersed in water, the tension will be released and the yarn will spring back to a much bulkier, shorter length than the original yarn. Neither the temperature of the water nor the method of washing is responsible; the yarn was deliberately processed to become bulky and to shrink, and knitted fabric made of it will be considerably smaller once washed than when first produced.

Yarns produced specifically for domestic textile crafts are heat-set at temperatures that will ensure that they do *not* react in the way just described when subjected to home laundering or ironing. Nevertheless, all yarns will show *some* reaction to laundering, but the reaction will be contained within reasonable limits.

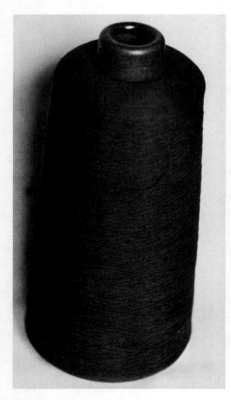

Fig. 2-7. *A cone of industrial nylon yarn.*

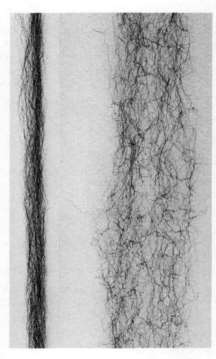

Fig. 2-8. *Left: a strand of nylon as it un-winds from the cone shown in figure 2-7. Right: the same yarn after it has been stretched and then released.*

Pilling

Pilling is the tendency of fibers to collect in small balls on the surface of a fabric (figure 2-9). Pilling is particularly common in loosely constructed materials, such as those knitted, crocheted, or loosely woven from yarns with a fuzzy surface. Loose fiber ends interlock with others, especially when the fabric is rubbed against itself during washing or wearing. Though many fibers have a tendency to pill, it is more of a problem with synthetic fibers, because their fiber strength makes them adhere to the yarn structure more tenaciously than the weaker, natural fibers do. Consequently, although a soft, short fiber, such as cashmere, may actually pill just as much as an acrylic, the pilling balls will fall off, whereas an acrylic fiber will be more likely to hold them in place.

Fig. 2-9. *The pilling balls can be seen on the surface of the fabric.*

Shrinkage

Fiber shrinkage is caused by several factors: friction, heat, relaxation, and steeping in water. Once these are distinguished from each other it is much easier to minimize shrinkage when laundering any type of fabric.

Friction   Friction, or rubbing, shrinkage is most prevalent in fibers, such as wool and hair, that are made up of scales running in one direction. When the fiber is moved or rubbed during washing or wearing, for example, the tendency is to move in the direction of least resistance; that is *with* and not against the scales. These then mass together and interlock, remaining fixed in this position and producing the well-known felted or matted look at underarms or other places subject to rubbing (figure 2-10). In fact, that is how felted fabric is made, and woven or knitted cloth can be felted by deliberately agitating the fabric in hot water. The more scaly the fibers, the

Fig. 2-10. *Felting at the underarm of a knitted garment; the scales in the fibers have interlocked and the fibers are matted together at that point.*

more likely this is to happen; the finer wools felt more than the coarser wools.

It is possible to launder wool with minimum friction shrinkage by allowing it to soak clean or gently squeezing it to remove dirt or stains rather than by rubbing it. Pure, untreated knitted wool garments can be unraveled, and the yarn reused, many years after they have first been knitted, provided the correct laundering procedure has always been followed.

Effect of Heat Fibers vary considerably in their reaction to heat. Linen, for example, is outstanding in its ability to cope with hot temperatures, whereas acrylics, at the other end of the scale, can only tolerate a small amount of heat.

Heat shrinkage affects all fibers; the important point here is not to exceed the heat level to which a particular fiber may be subjected. Synthetics are known for their resistance to shrinkage. As indicated earlier, however, this is only true if the original heat-set temperature of the fibers is not exceeded in laundering or ironing. Excess heat can both weaken and disintegrate fibers, so considerable care is needed in the laundering and ironing processes for fibers that can only tolerate low heat levels. All fibers have optimum temperatures that should not be exceeded when laundering (see table 3).

A further point worth bearing in mind is that fluctuations of temperature in the washing and rinsing waters may also cause problems with shrinkage.

Table 3. Safe Washing and Ironing Temperatures

Ironing:	Cool: 110°C 230°F	Warm: 150°C 300°F	Hot: 180°C 350°F	Very Hot: 200°C 400°F
FIBER TYPE				
Acetate		X		
Acrylics	X			
Cotton				X
Linen				X
Nylon		X		
Polyester		X		
Rayon			X	
Silk		X		
Wool		X		
Washing:	Cool: 30°C 80°F	Warm: 40°C 100°F	Hot: 60°C 190°F	Very Hot: 90°C 200°F

Blends: Always use the lower category temperature for blends.

Steeping in Water Many fibers absorb water easily and swell in size, becoming considerably thicker in cross section but not becoming appreciably longer. As they are held in the yarn structure by the manufacturing processes, the thickening of the fiber leads to a shortening of the yarn length (figure 2-11). The fabric made of such fibers will dry to this shape unless "ironed out," something which is not necessarily a good idea for all types of fabric construction. However, the initial shrinkage is the most significant; after the first wash, most yarns remain relatively stable.

Relaxation Relaxation shrinkage is not often mentioned, although the nylon yarn pictured in figure 2-8 is a good example of an excessive reaction. Any fiber is subject to a certain amount of this shrinkage. Fibers are spun and finished to make yarns. Spinning and finishing processes tend to stretch and set the yarns, and they are even more strained after winding onto packages or into balls, which again adds tension. Processing the yarn into a fabric may add yet another strain, more pronounced in some methods of crafting than in others. When the material is then wetted many of these various tensions are released, and the yarn reverts to a "relaxed" stage. It is not, therefore, so much a question of shrinkage as a question of change of shape. The original shape of some suitable fabrics can be ironed or steam-pressed back again. It is here that the difference between knitting and weaving is shown to a considerable degree: domestically knitted fabric is not as suitable for ironing or pressing processes as woven fabric. A

Fig. 2-11.
Left: cotton yarn before steeping in water. Right: the same cotton yarn after steeping in water and drying.

domestically knitted fabric structure is easily distorted by the heat and pressure of ironing, whatever the fiber content of the yarn used to make the fabrics a woven structure is not nearly as easily distorted. It is always a good idea to make a trial fabric swatch of reasonable size and to allow the yarn to relax before measuring the fabric tension.

Durability

Making a beautiful fabric can be very time-consuming. It is important to know what will make the fabric last, perhaps for your own lifetime and beyond. A sheer lace must be made of fine lace yarn, but one that is tough enough to withstand the ravages of time (figure 2-12).

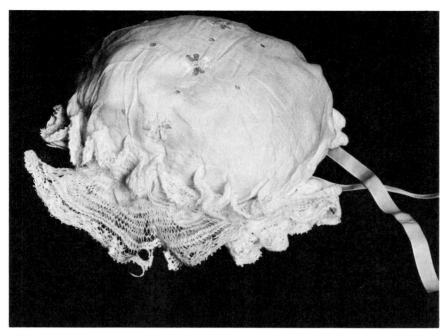

Fig. 2-12. *This delightful bonnet has remained in good condition except for the knitted lace border; a better yarn would last longer.*

Strength
Assuming the same thickness of yarn, a relatively elastic one will not break as quickly as an inelastic one, even if the actual tensile (pulling) strengths are the same. This means that, in practice, an elastic yarn can be as useful as a much stronger but inelastic one. In fact, some yarns—nylon, for example—are both strong and elastic.

Hot or Cold Strength
As already mentioned, temperatures affect fibers. They may become brittle with too much heat, or they may soften and lengthen to such an extent that they break easily. This means that some yarns, and consequently some fabrics, may not revert to their original shape after laundering.

Light
Light may affect the fiber itself, not just the color the fiber has been dyed. Yarns chosen to be used to make home furnishings need to be relatively resistant to the effects of light, and clothes worn in areas with much sunlight may also be affected.

The effect of light is not the same on all fibers; some, such as polyester, are degraded only by the ultraviolet rays in light; others, such as cotton, are affected by all light. Where ultraviolet light is not intense, such as in the temperate climatic zones, polyester resists sunlight much better than nylon does. Polyester curtains, for instance, will last longer than nylon ones.

Mildew
Mildew, a weakening and unsightly fungus, can be a problem for fibers stored in damp conditions. Generally, the synthetic fibers are immune to damage by mildew, though it may appear on the surface of fabrics made of them. Regenerated (see chapter 6) and natural fibers can, however, be badly affected. Fabrics and yarns should be stored in reasonably dry conditions, though a small amount of moisture is necessary to prevent fibers from becoming too brittle and thus deteriorating.

Moths
The female clothes moth lays eggs in a dark, warm place where there will be food for her hatched larvae. Wool fibers, for instance, contain such food. The larvae also eat other hair and sometimes silk, but cannot digest synthetic or cellulosic fibers. Mixed fiber yarns containing wool or hair may also be attacked. Many wools are now automatically mothproof, but specialist wools, such as Shetland or Cretan wool, may not have been treated and should be stored with some type of moth repellent or killer.

3/ Natural Fibers: Wool

There are three sources of natural fibers: the coat or covering growing from the skin of many animals, the filaments spun by silkworms for their cocoons, and the leaf, stalk, or seedpod of various plants. At one time the coat of domestic sheep, bred primarily to produce a fine, soft, white, crimpy (curly) fiber, rather than the long hairs usually associated with animal coats, was the most important textile fiber in the world. However, the introduction of cotton to the U.S. and Britain and the invention and modifications of man-made fibers have greatly reduced the use of wool fiber. In fact, the latest figures show wool to represent only a part of 1 percent of U.S. fiber mill consumption, whereas in 1940 the figure was as high as 9 percent. During the same period cotton has fallen from 81 percent of consumption to only 29 percent, while man-made fibers have risen from 10 to 70 percent of fiber mill consumption.

Natural fibers do still have advantages over synthetic ones for some purposes, and although it is neither practicable nor even desirable to revert to purely natural fibers (since this would involve using a very large acreage to graze animals or grow plants), many crafters prefer to use yarns made of natural fibers for their textile projects.

The most important natural fiber for domestic hand- and machine-knitting and weaving is undoubtedly wool. Pure wool yarn is not always easy to purchase in the ordinary yarn store, but several specialist suppliers, some of whom are listed at the end of this book, are able to offer not only pure wool, but specialist and hand-spun wools. Examples are Vermont grown wool (figure 3-1), Icelandic Lopi wool, and Shetland wool. Wool

Fig. 3-1.
A lock of Dorset Horn wool.

31

fiber is making a comeback because it has characteristics that may have been approximated by some man-made fibers, but that have not yet been matched or exceeded. Wool is also a delightful yarn to craft with.

At one time everyone knew the reasons why wool is such an outstanding textile fiber. Now these reasons are not so clear, and a brief explanation of what wool is and some of the qualities which make it such a popular choice among contemporary crafters should be useful.

The Meaning of the Word *Wool*

The fibers that make up the fleece (the covering) of sheep are known as wool. Although other animal hair has similar characteristics, it is simpler to refer to these other hair fibers by names such as cashmere, mohair, and so on. (These fibers will be discussed in the next chapter.) Generally, animal coats are composed of an undercoat of fine, crimpy fibers and an outer coat of longer, less crimpy ones. The undercoat of some animals other than sheep, such as cashmere, may legally be termed *wool*, but in this book the word will be added to the fiber name to distinguish it from both the longer, outer hairs of that animal and from sheep's wool.

Another meaning of the word *wool* is in the sense of woolen yarn; again, the word is assumed to mean a yarn made from sheep's wool. The word *woolen* also has two meanings; the one used here is simply descriptive of the yarn fiber content. The other meaning (fully discussed in chapter 6) refers to a particular method of spinning yarn.

Sheep

Sheep were domesticated many thousands of years ago by the nomadic tribes living in the Near East (Asia Minor and the Arabian Peninsula). The wild sheep, known as Mouflon (figure 3-2), looks more like a small deer than a sheep and has a tan colored covering and the double coat associated with most animal hair coverings. The very soft undercoat molts during the spring. However, man has bred the sheep selectively for a light-colored fiber that resembles the undercoat, rather than the long hairs of the top coat. In fact the selective breeding has modified the long hairs until they approximate the undercoat fibers. These hairs do *not* molt, so the modern sheep has a continuously growing coat that can, and must, be shorn (cut off; figure 3-3). Shearing ensures that the whole fleece is harvested, but it also means that the sheep is dependent on man for removing the fleece. Otherwise it would, for the most part, stay on the sheep's back, becoming a tangled, filthy, matted covering which would eventually kill the sheep. Shetland sheep are an exception; they still retain the original characteristic molt and the fleece is "rooed" (plucked or combed) from the animal. The rooing has to be timed carefully so that the whole fleece is salvaged.

Although shearing can, in theory, be done at any time, in practice it is done in the spring after the first "rise" (spring growth) of new hair. The fibers grow weaker in winter and tend to mat into a dense mass not easily penetrated by the shears whereas the new growth, nearest the skin, is easily cut. The animal can also manage without its coat in the spring.

Fig. 3-2.
A Mouflon sheep, photo-
graphed at the London
Zoo. (Photo: Jeremy
Warburg)

Fig. 3-3. Center: pure Polled Dorset ewe with lamb. Left and right: Clun (crossbred) ewes.
Note the difference in length between the ewes' and the lamb's fleece. (Photo: Jeremy
Warburg)

Breeds of Sheep

There are over one thousand breeds of sheep raised for both wool and meat and sometimes a combination of the two. The Merino, which is said .to have originated in North Africa, but was imported to Spain and then to France, was eventually bred into the sheep that produces the finest, most consistent, and most crimpy overall fleece. There are several types of Merino sheep; the Delaine Merino is the breed favored in the U.S. Another fine breed containing Merino blood is the Rambouillet, which originally came from France. Wool "quality" is graded relative to the best Merino wool, and table 4 gives the U.S. "blood" classifications, the equivalent worsted count numbers (explained in chapter 7), and the latest micron measurements. The finest wool fibers can be spun to a 100s worsted count, but any wool with a quality count of between 64s and 48s may be used for domestic crafts.

It would be a mistake to think that only Merino wool is valuable; many other wools and wool blends are useful for particular purposes.

Table 4. Wool Grades or Quality

Blood	Worsted Count	Microns
Full blood	100s	Under 17
Fine	80s, 70s, 64s	19, 21, 22
Half blood	62s, 60s, 58s	23, 25, 26
Three-eighths blood	56s	27
Quarter blood	50s, 48s	30, 32
Low-quarter blood	46s	34
Common	44s	36
Braid	40s, 36s, 30s	40 or over

Fiber Characteristics

A sheep's fleece consists of three types of fiber: the undercoat, or wool fibers; the outer coat, or hair fibers, that are made up of longer, thicker fibers than wool; and the kemp hairs. Kemps are the coarse, chalky white hairs that molt within a short time.

Fiber Structure

The fiber structure of wool (figure 3-4) can be seen as overlapping scales pointing towards the tip. The fibers can readily slide forward, but the scales interlock if the direction is reversed. Some fibers are much scalier than others both within the same fleece and, particularly, between different breeds of sheep.

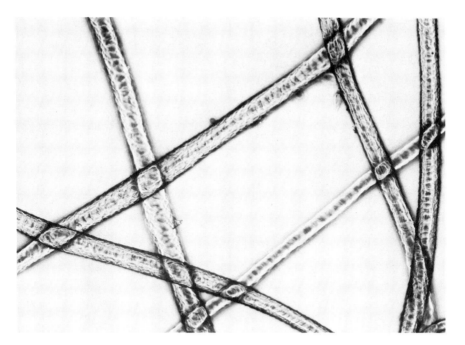

Fig. 3-4. *The scales in the wool fiber will interlock at points of intersection. (Photo: Richard Warburg)*

The structure of wool consists of: the medulla (hollow core), which takes up most of the kemp fibers, but also exists in other hair fibers, as well as some wool fibers (very fine undercoat fibers may not have a medulla at all); the cortex (core), which consists of spindle-shaped cells that provide the elasticity and resilience of wool; and the cuticle (outer layer), which has the scalelike structure.

The fiber has a pointed tip when it first grows, but fibers from previously shorn sheep have two cut ends. Because it sheds naturally, kemp has a tapered end and a frayed root end.

Fiber Diameter or Width
The undercoat fiber of the wild sheep is finer than the finest Merino fiber. Mouflon fiber averages about 15 microns (millionth part of a meter), which is about 1/1700 inch. The average Merino fiber is 24 microns, and wool fibers of this thickness are regarded as of Merino quality, although they may not always come from Merino sheep (figure 3-5).

Medium fibers are roughly 40 microns and the outer hair fibers roughly 80 microns. These thicker fibers are also longer and their thickness varies along the length. Kemp will be even thicker and shorter than the other fibers (figure 3-6).

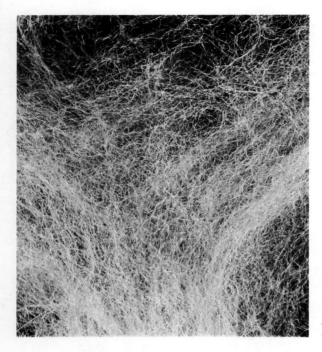

Fig. 3-5.
Lamb's wool fibers; lamb's wool is always finer than wool from fully grown animals, of whatever breed.

Fig. 3-6.
The kemp fibers are the thicker, white fibers among the dark-gray Herdwick fibers.

Staple Length

Wool staple is judged by the length of various "locks" into which the sheep's fleece falls naturally. Figure 3-7 shows eight different types of staple from different breeds of sheep; the length is taken from the cut end to the taper. Each lock will contain different lengths of wool and hair fiber and may also contain hair and kemp. Merino sheep have a fairly uniform staple, although the quality tends to vary between different parts of the fleece, as with other sheep. Fibers may vary widely within the fleece and are normally graded from best to worst starting from the shoulders and progressing through the sides, neck, back, haunch, and belly, to the legs, tail, and face.

Fig. 3-7. *Reading from left to right, top to bottom, the eight illustrated locks are: Wensleydale, Rough Fell, Devon Longwool, Cotswold, Southdown, Dorset Horn, Romney Marsh, and Herdwick.*

Color

Although sheep are bred to obtain the lightest fiber color so that wool can readily be bleached and dyed to light shades, some breeds do produce several "natural" colors. These are called "black wool," and such wool is often prized for making woven or knitted fabric in various shades of undyed gray or brown (figure 3-8).

The staple tip of a colored fleece usually fades considerably during the season. Figure 3-9 shows a Shetland moorit (tan color) fleece that is quite pale at the top. The base of the staple may also become paler in winter, both because the fleece will grow more slowly then and the available food will be of lower quality.

Wool that has been dyed will show faults that "natural"-colored wool

Fig. 3-8. *Knitted bolero vest made from hand-spun Jacob fleece of different colors.*

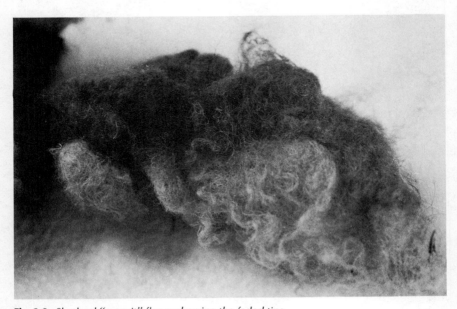

Fig. 3-9. *Shetland "moorit" fleece showing the faded tips.*

Fig. 3-10. *Kemp hairs showing up in Swaledale fibers.*

may hide. Kemp, for instance, is so hollow that it does not take up dye as easily as the other fibers in the fleece and will, therefore, stand out as lighter colored (figure 3-10). Pulled wool (wool taken from slaughtered animals) may have damaged root ends that take dye up more readily, thus giving an uneven color to the wool. Badly sorted wool will contain unevenly dyed fibers.

Crimp
One of the important features of wool is its crimp or curl. This is sometimes called waviness, but the crimp is not simply a wave along the fiber length. Crimp winds in a spiral and can readily be seen in the locks (figures 3-11 and 3-12).

One of the effects of the crimp in wool is that it produces a lofty (air-pocketed) yarn. In fact, even the tightest spun worsted (see chapter 6) contains 60 percent volume of air.

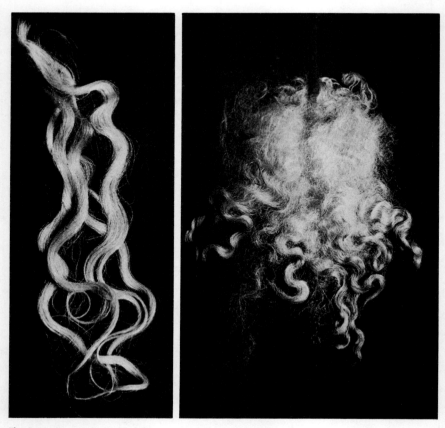

Fig. 3-11. *Devon Longwool does not have much crimp.*   **Fig. 3-12.** *Cotswold is a fairly crimpy wool fiber.*

Warmth and Insulation

There are several reasons why wool is warm to wear. Both the scaliness of the fiber and its crimp contribute to air pockets along the length of woolen yarn, and trapped, still air is an excellent insulator. These properties of wool fiber explain how sheep can exist in icy conditions without feeling unduly cold and in hot desert conditions without feeling unduly hot. Wool garments, too, protect from both direct heat and cold.

Another reason for the warmth of wool is, as already mentioned, its ability to give out heat when wet. Air-dry wool contains some water, but wool can absorb up to 30 percent moisture before it begins to feel wet. As the wool absorbs this moisture, heat is actually given off, and body warmth will not be lost in evaporating this moisture. That is why wool is such an outstanding fiber for damp, cold climates and why synthetic fibers cannot yet compete with wool.

Categories of Wool

It is difficult for the consumer to know whether a wool yarn is of good quality just by looking at it. In order to help the consumer, the International Wool Secretariat has introduced the "Woolmark" (figure 3-13). Certain wool yarns are allowed to display the Woolmark label, signifying that these wool yarns reach certain standards, which include, as well as fiber content, properties such as colorfastness, and shrinkage and abrasion resistance. The intention is to ensure that any wool yarn that carries the Woolmark label is of a high enough standard for that particular category of wool.

Fig. 3-13. *Label displaying the Woolmark (right).*

When applied to yarns, the Woolmark is applied only to yarns made of pure new wool, but not to *all* such yarns. The reason is quite simply that yarn can be described as pure new wool and yet be of a quite inferior standard.

The following classifications define certain categories according to U.S. government standards:

Virgin Wool, Pure New Wool

Virgin wool and pure new wool must refer to wool that is wholly new wool and has never been used before in any process whatsoever.

Wool

Wool refers to new wool or wool fibers reclaimed from scraps, broken threads, or noils (short fibers left from combing wool preparatory to worsted spinning) used in the production of wool yarns.

Reprocessed Wool
Wool that has been previously used in making a textile material. Garnetted (shredded back to fibrous state) scraps and various clippings from woven, felted, or knitted sample swatches or fabrics may be used to make "reprocessed" wool.

Reused Wool, Shoddy
Shoddy is wool that has been reclaimed from previously used or worn materials made of wool. Reused wool may be made from old, pure wool clothing, waste from wool manufacturing, and rags of all kinds.

It is important to realize that not all reprocessed or reused products are bad in themselves. Yarns made from such products may be useful for special purposes.

Special Wools
There are a number of special category wools which are often mentioned. The following is a list of the most common ones.

Lamb's Wool
The first fleece sheared from a lamb about six to eight months old is known as lamb's wool or fleece wool, whatever the breed of sheep the wool came from. The fibers are tapered because the ends have never been clipped before; the wool is of fine, soft, very resilient quality, although not as strong as wool from a fully grown animal (see figure 3-5).

Hogget Wool
Hogget wool comes from sheep about twelve to fourteen months old that have not been shorn before. They, too, have fibers with tapered ends. Hogget is stronger than lamb's wool, yet still of high quality, and is often used to make warp yarns.

Pulled Wool
Wool taken from a dead lamb or sheep slaughtered for meat is called pulled wool. It is obtained by sweating (heating the pelt until the wool is loosened) or by using a chemical applied to the pelt. The wool is inferior because sheep raised primarily for their meat do not necessarily have a high-quality wool. Also, the roots of the fibers may be damaged by the chemicals used or by the force used in pulling the fibers from the pelt.

Dead Wool (Murrain)
Dead wool is wool taken from sheep that have died from accidents while on the farm. It is of inferior quality.

Kempy Wool
Kemp, the coarse, strong, relatively straight, chalky white fiber, is particularly prevalent in the fleece of some sheep. Kempy wool may not appeal for all purposes, but it can give a distinctive look to tweeds, say, and it is also very strong (figures 3-6 and 3-10).

Machine Washable Wool, Superwash Wool

Superwash is the name often given to wools treated to make them shrink resistant and machine washable. The scaly fibers are coated with a plastic resin to smooth them out. This type of wool can then be washed at a special setting in some washing machines, but it does lose something of the stretch and feel of untreated wool. Rib-knitted fabrics, for instance, no longer have that special elasticity. The yarn is relatively slippery, and great care must be taken to sew in all loose ends in crafted work.

Oiled Wool

Wool fibers may be spun in oil because the different industrial processes used to prepare them for spinning remove the natural lanolin (sheep's grease). Some hand spinners, however, spin wool "in the raw"; the lanolin is then still in the wool. Lanolin, soft and pliable shortly after shearing, becomes brittle with age, and has a distinct odor that is not to everyone's taste.

Most wools sold for crafting are "scoured" (cleaned) of any spinning oil before sale, but some wool is specially treated to be water-repellent. This type of wool is often termed oiled "Aran" wool, though it may not actually come from the islands (in Galway Bay off Ireland) of that name.

Some industrial wool may be sold with the spinning oil still in it; such yarn can be woven or knitted as it is and the oil scoured out of the finished fabric. Crafting with oiled wool is easy because the lubricant makes the yarn slippery, but several points need to be borne in mind. The wool is weighed with the oil in it and so part of the weight you pay for is oil; the yarn can be very greasy; and the oil can have quite a pungent odor. The wool may also be deceptive to work with; a thin, stringy yarn may become soft and fluffy after scouring (figure 3-14). Allowance has to be made for this possibility before knitting or weaving with such yarn.

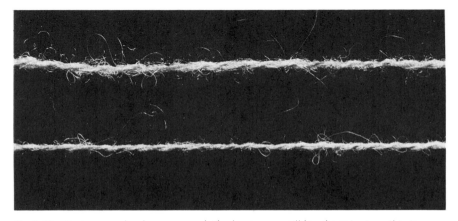

Fig. 3-14. *The top yarn has been scoured; the lower yarn still has the spinning oil in it.*

Cheviots

Hard-spun (tightly twisted) singles yarns, originally made of wool from a breed of sheep called Cheviot, are used primarily for tweeds (figure 3-15).

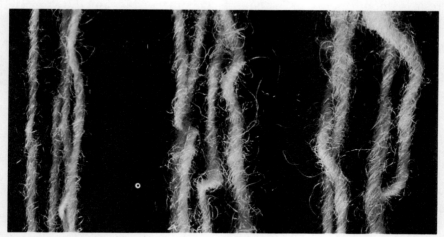

Fig. 3-15. *Hard-twist singles, in three thicknesses, spun from Cheviot wool.*

Zephyr Yarn

Zephyr yarn is spun on the worsted system (see chapter 6) from wool fibers of 64s grade or better.

Named Wools

A few wools are sold by the name of the breed of sheep or the area they come from.

Herdwick Wool

The yarn from the fleece of the semiwild flocks of Herdwick sheep in Cumbria (Northern England) is very tough. The natural colors vary from almost black through shades of gray to almost white. There is a fairly high kemp content in the fleece, but, as the yarn is sold blended from the various natural grays, the kemps do not show up particularly well and merely give the yarn strength. It is said that John Peel's "coat so gray" was made of Herdwick wool.

Icelandic Wool, Lopi Wool

Icelandic wool comes from a breed of sheep that thrives in the Arctic regions of Iceland and feeds on the sparse vegetation there. The fleece consists of a soft undercoat and much tougher outer hair. The wool is particularly soft and resilient, as well as extremely rugged. The yarn is sold as roving or as a bulky singles yarn in various shades of undyed colors ranging from off white to dark brown, as well as some dyed colors (figure 3-16).

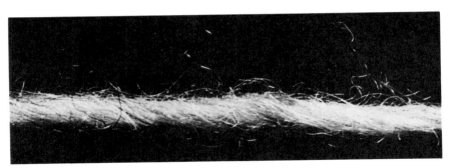

Fig. 3-16. *Icelandic Lopi singles.*

Jacob Wool

The Jacob is a piebald sheep and has hereditary white markings among the colored wool. The thin face and the four horns give it a rather goatlike look. Its name comes from its resemblance to sheep mentioned in Genesis. Jacob asked his father-in-law, Laban, to allow him to own the sheep and goats of "divers colors" he had separated from the rest of the herds; these piebald animals thrived so well that Jacob became rich and was able to leave Laban's employ. Joseph, Jacob's favorite son, wore a "coat of many colors," said to have been made of the different wool colors found in the fleece of Jacob's sheep.

Although at one time the Jacob sheep had become very rare, it is now popular with amateur sheep breeders. The wool (often homespun) is sold by specialist suppliers. Figure 3-17 shows the typical Jacob markings on a crossbred ewe.

Fig. 3-17.
Crossbred Jacob ewe with twin, crossbred lambs. (Photo: Jeremy Warburg)

Shetland Wool

Real Shetland is a woolen yarn spun to the Galashiels cut (see chapter 7) and made from the fleece of sheep raised in the Shetland and Orkney Isles, off Scotland. The original Shetland was a very small animal. The lamb was so small that it could shelter from the cold in a rabbit's burrow. Recently, however, the sheep have been allowed to interbreed with imported Cheviot and Blackface, so pure Shetland wool is now hard to obtain.

High-quality Shetland wool is readily available from specialist suppliers. The yarn thickness (measured in plies) is very misleading as it is *not* spun to the worsted count (see chapter 7). Shetland-type yarns are often sold as mill ends from industrial processes, and this wool is often of inferior grade though very inexpensive (figure 3-18). The wool is usually sold "in the oil" and is useful for hand-knitting or as a weft yarn. It is not strong enough to be used as a warp yarn and may break easily when used for machine-knitting. Garments made from such yarn are not as hard-wearing as one might like.

Fig. 3-18.
The inside of the yarn support shows that the yarn is a "Shetland-type" wool, not a genuine Shetland wool.

Wool for Textile Crafts

Wool is available in a large range of quality, color, and finish. Hand-knitters and crocheters can use very soft-spun, even unspun, wool, and weavers can incorporate this type of yarn in the weft for unusual effects. Machine-knitters, on the other hand, need yarn that is strong enough to withstand the strains of machine-knitting. Softly spun, poor-quality wool may not be strong enough. Warp yarns for weavers will also have to be of adequate quality and strength.

Generally, knitters need to look for wools of 58s to 54s quality and a staple length from 1½ to 6 inches (3 to 15 cm.). Crimp, softness, and lack of kemp are also desirable except for knits that are to be used as rugged outerwear.

For woven goods, yarn strength may well be more important than yarn softness. Warp yarns definitely need to be strong enough to withstand the tension put on them by being set on a loom. Weft yarns need to be able to withstand the pressure put on them by being "beaten-in" (pushed against the already formed cloth): a soft knitting fingering might be beaten out of recognition! This is not to say that knitting wools cannot be used for weaving but that, in general, they are not particularly suitable. The finer yarns often required in weaving are also stronger when made of the 56s to 48s qualities with a medium staple of 4 to 5 inches (10 to 15 cm.). Crimp is still desirable in such yarns, and kemp may actually be an advantage—when making tweed, for example.

4/ Natural Fibers: Cotton, Hair, Linen, and Silk

Although wool is the most important, and probably the most popular, of the natural fibers used by textile crafters, cotton comes a close second to it. Hair from animals other than sheep is also becoming more and more popular, particularly in mixed fiber yarns. But perhaps the most exciting development is the resurgence of silk yarn. This is at present available from a few sources only, but gaining in popularity all the time.

Cotton

Cotton fiber comes from the hairs of the seedpod of a plant of the Mallow family, of the genus *Gossypium*. The fiber is formed by the downy substance around the outer coat of the seed (figure 4-1). Considerable variation exists among cotton fibers, depending on the variety of plant grown, the soil, and the climate where it is grown. Quality may also be affected by weather conditions and insect damage in a given season.

Cotton is known to have been used as a textile fiber for at least three thousand years and may have been used more than seven thousand years ago. Evidence of cotton cultivation comes from India and Peru, but the fiber was not introduced to Europe until the thirteenth century, when the returning Crusaders are said to have brought it back with them from the Near East. Although the plant was known on the North American continent by the end of the fifteenth century, cotton was not planted there commercially until the beginning of the seventeenth century.

The wool industry in England first felt the need to protect itself against imports of cotton from North America in the late seventeenth century. By the beginning of the eighteenth century, laws were passed forbidding the spinning and weaving of cotton in Britain, since the spinning of the imported cotton fiber was seen as a threat to the more expensive, but indigenous, wool fiber. Eventually these laws had to be abandoned, and cotton spinning became one of the major industrial enterprises in Britain as well as in the United States. It was the growth of "King Cotton" that encouraged the expansion of slave labor for picking the cotton bolls when the fiber was ripe for harvesting. Cotton is no longer king, but roughly a fifth of textile mill consumption in the U.S. is still cotton.

Both the staple length and the basic fiber color of cotton vary considerably. Staple length ranges from the very short (not over ¾ inch or 2 cm.) to the extra long (up to 2½ inches or 10 cm.). The fiber color ranges from almost white to a dark brown. The whiter the original fiber, the less bleaching and consequent weakening of the fiber is required.

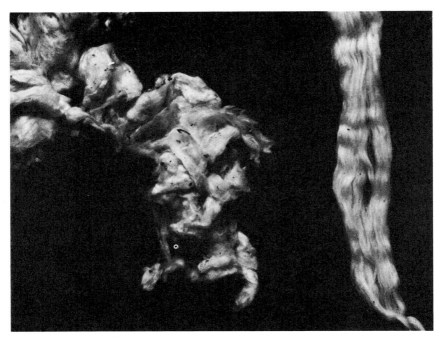

Fig. 4-1. *Left: cotton fiber. Right: cotton sliver.*

Some high-quality cottons are well known and a few of their characteristics are described here.

Sea Island Cotton
Sea Island cotton was first grown on an island of that name off Georgia, but it is now also grown in the central states of the U.S., in the West Indies, and in Mexico. It is a long-stapled, almost white cotton.

Egyptian Cotton
A variety of Egyptian cotton, called Sakel, is lustrous, cream-colored, and of good staple length. Other Egyptian cottons, though long-stapled and of good quality, are brown or dark brown in color and require heavy bleaching.

Pima Cotton
Pima is a fine, white, lustrous, and strong cotton fiber of uniform long-staple length grown in the U.S. and Bolivia. This cotton was first cultivated in Pima, Arizona, from Egyptian cottonseed.

American Upland Cotton
The bulk of the U.S. cotton crop consists of American Upland cotton. Some of this fiber is fairly white, but it has a shorter staple length and is less lustrous and weaker than the high quality cottons mentioned above.

Far Eastern Cottons
Indian and Chinese cottons have short staple lengths and are relatively coarse and dull.

It is important to realize that there are very considerable differences in cotton; cotton yarn prices can range from very cheap to very expensive. There is an easy test for strength: if you can tear the yarn easily it is of inferior quality. Such yarn may still be a good choice for some textile projects. It may be short-sighted, however, to use such cottons for warp yarns, for laces, or for fine sewing threads that depend for their strength on the fine, long staple and the mild amount of bleaching needed to make them white.

Undyed cotton yarns are often offered. These yarns can certainly be of high quality, and for textile projects where beige and brown colors are suitable, they can be good buys. It is wise to test all cotton yarns for strength before use, as so many textile projects involving cotton are time-consuming, and the result is meant to be long lasting (figure 4-2). It is possible to bleach undyed cotton at home. However, although cotton may safely be bleached with ordinary household products, sodium hypochlorite may cause yellowing through overconcentration of the chemical, or because the cotton yarn contains a chlorine retentive finish (figure 4-3).

Fig. 4-2. *A beautiful and time-consuming lace, hand-knitted in a cotton crochet yarn.*

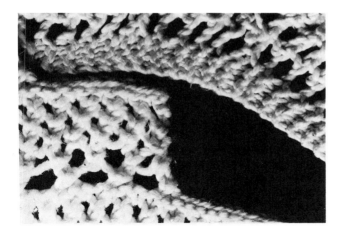

Fig. 4-3.
The gray part of the illustration shows yellowing of a bleached cotton fabric.

Fiber Characteristics
The cotton fiber is relatively strong because of the construction of the fiber itself. The internal structure is crossed with spiraling fibrils, and these have the effect of producing a twisted strand that interlocks readily with other cotton fibers (figure 4-4). There are no overlapping scales such as the ones found in wool. Cotton is a smooth fiber, and the process of "mercerization" (passing the fiber through caustic soda and washing this out under tension) considerably increases the luster, strength, and affinity to many dyes.

Yarn strength is determined by the length of the staple, the amount of twist, and the fact that many cotton yarns are cabled (figure 4-5 and see chapter 6). Compact fabric construction produced by weaving with yarns

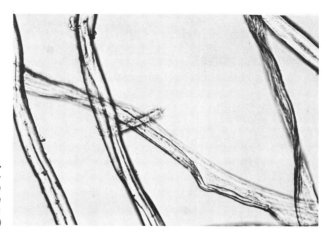

Fig. 4-4.
Magnified cotton fibers. Note the smooth surface and the twist in the fiber. (Photo: Richard Warburg)

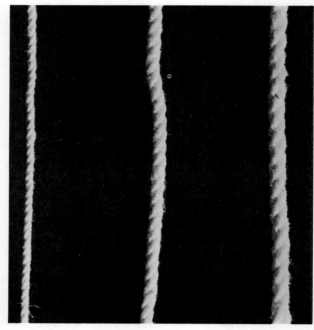

Fig. 4-5.
*Three thicknesses of
cabled cotton.*

of a high count (see chapter 7) will lead to very strong fabrics. Only the best cottons should be used for fragile fabrics such as laces and sheer woven goods (figure 4-6).

Cotton increases in strength when it is wet. Once the outer layer of the fiber is broken down by mercerizing, or by other finishing processes, the fiber becomes very absorbent. A low-twisted yarn will be more absorbent than a high-twisted one because the fibers will be held less tightly in the yarn structure and can, therefore, expand more easily. *Fabric* structure will also affect absorbency, so that a loosely knitted fabric will be much more absorbent than a tightly woven one. Loop fabrics are particularly absorbent.

Cotton will shrink a great deal in any fabric construction, and the first laundering will set it to a more stable shape. Laundering is a good "pre-shrinking" treatment for any textile project.

There is very little elasticity or resilience in cotton fiber. It is an excellent conductor of heat, and this, together with its absorptive qualities, makes cotton a comfortable fiber to wear in hot climates. Light tends to yellow cotton and it mildews easily, however. Cotton is not affected by moths, but, if a yarn or fabric is a mixture of wool and cotton, the yarn structure may be susceptible to moth damage.

Yarns can be spun to cotton counts of 400 (see chapter 7), but yarns of a fortieth of this value are fine enough for most crochet, weaving, or lace-making projects.

Fig. 4-6. *This detail of a 150-year-old robe shows cotton used for weaving the basic fabric as well as for making two types of handmade lace.*

Hair

Although wool is the most important of the animal coat fibers, a number of other animal coats yield fibers that are excellent for textile crafts. Some of these fibers belong to the luxury class, as the animals they are taken from produce only a small amount of useful fiber each year. Other animal hairs are readily available. Many of these fibers are well known and extensively used. The characteristics of animal hair fibers are similar to wool, but one special characteristic of such fibers is that they give more warmth for less weight than do sheep wool fibers. The special animal-coat hairs that are generally available in yarns sold for textile crafts are very often blends of the expensive, undercoat hairs of several species of the camel, cow, goat, and rabbit families mixed together with lamb's wool. The softness of lamb's wool does not detract from the soft "feel" of the speciality fibers as much as sheep's wool might. Adding lamb's wool helps to make the expensive fibers go farther. The label on the yarn package should show the amount of the "named" fiber in percentage terms. It is useful to know that the word *type* often follows a fiber name. Yarns labeled in this way may be perfectly good yarns, but the speciality fiber name on the yarn package may be misleading to the uninitiated. It pays to study the label carefully. It is possible to buy 100 percent mohair yarn; it is also possible to buy a mohair-type yarn that has only a 5 percent mohair content.

The Camel Family
Several cameloid animals produce excellent textile fibers.

Alpaca The alpaca is related to the llama and lives in the higher regions of the Andes. The most prized fiber comes from the Suri breed of alpaca. The staple is relatively long, from 6 to 11 inches (15 to 26 cm.). Although the structure of the fiber is similar to wool—and the fiber may be termed wool for labeling purposes—the scales are not as pronounced as in wool. Consequently, the fiber is more lustrous, and yarns made of it have a silky sheen. The fiber is water-repellent and has a high insulating power. Natural colors range from the deepest black to the very lightest soft white (figure 4-7). As the fiber is hard to bleach, much alpaca is sold in natural, undyed colors. Fiber quality varies appreciably, as seen in the illustration: the kempy fiber mass, second from left, contrasts with the smooth, untangled masses on either side of it. Alpaca fibers mixed with wool may be offered in dyed colors, although dyed pure alpaca yarns can sometimes be found.

Fig. 4-7. *Five "natural" alpaca fiber colors. Note the high kemp content of the second fiber mass from the left.*

Llama The llama is a pack animal originating in the higher regions of the Andes. Although llama fiber is fairly coarse, it is valuable for mixing with alpaca fibers, especially with the reddish brown, rarer alpaca fibers that it sometimes replaces. It is easy to distinguish llama fiber from pure alpaca fiber because it has a much less lustrous look and a less silky feel. Llama fiber has high insulative quality, colorfastness, and good durability (figure 4-8).

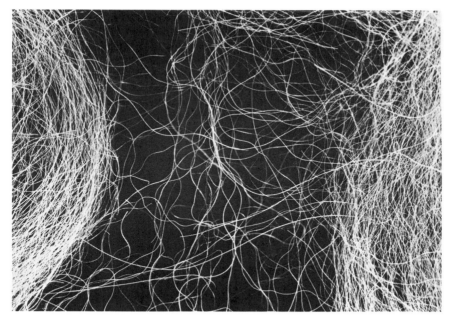

Fig. 4-8. *Llama fiber.*

Guanaco The guanaco is related to the alpaca and llama, is primarily undomesticated, and comes from southern Argentina. Guanaco fiber is very fine and silky; its color ranges from reddish brown through honey beige to the finest white, and it is lightweight, resilient, warm, and rather expensive.

Vicuna The vicuna is a rare, wild relative of the alpaca, found at the higher altitudes in the Andes. Vicuna fiber is the softest and most delicate of the camel-family fibers and has good elasticity and resilience. The fiber has a silky luster, is exceptionally soft to handle, and is one of the highest priced fibers on the market. The length of the staple is around 1½ inches (4 cm.), and the fiber diameter averages 13 microns— even|finer than cashmere. Vicuna fiber is spun into yarn on the woolen system (see chapter 6).

Camel Hair The underhair of the two-humped Bactrian camel is lustrous and extremely soft. The color ranges from light tan to brownish black, and the fiber may be classified as wool. The staple is very short.

Goat Family
Goats and sheep belong to the same family. Some of the finest textile fibers are obtained from goats.

Cashmere Cashmere goats come from the Himalayan mountain re-gions and comprise several breeds. The undercoat fibers are combed from the animal—the goats are not shorn. Cashmere staple ranges from 1¼ to 3½ inches (3 to 8 cm.) and the fiber diameter ranges from just under 15 microns to nearly 18 microns, depending on the breed of goat. Cashmere is a very fine, soft fiber with few and far apart scales (figure 4-9). The fibers have a wonderfully soft feel and can be worn next to the skin without discomfort.

The biggest disadvantage of choosing cashmere is its high price. The characteristic fiber color ranges from black through brown and gray to white, and, although cashmere is not as strong as wool, it is warmer, weight for weight (figure 4-10).

Yarns containing cashmere are often sold with the spinning oil still in them. It is important to make the fabric structure loose enough to allow for considerable expansion of the yarn after scouring.

Fig. 4-9.
Cashmere fibers.

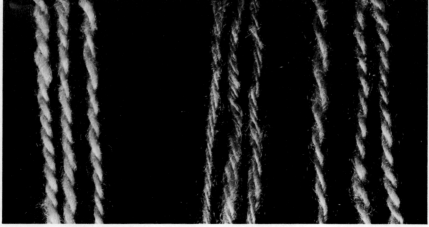

Fig. 4-10. *"Natural-colored" cashmere yarns.*

Mohair Mohair is the name given to the long outer hairs of the fleece of the angora goat. This animal was originally bred in Ankara (Turkey), but is now also bred extensively in South Africa and the U.S. The hair can be shorn once or twice a year. A staple of 9 to 12 inches (20 to 30 cm.) is obtained from a full year's growth and a staple of 8 to 10 inches (17 to 25 cm.) is obtained if the animal is shorn twice a year. The kemp content of the fiber can be high, a disadvantage, as kempy fiber does not process as readily or take up dye as easily as kemp-free fiber.

Mohair fiber is very strong and resilient (figure 4-11). Its light, usually white color can be dyed to any shade, including delicate pastel colors. The smooth fiber does not attract dirt easily and has an alluring, lustrous sheen. Like other hair fibers, mohair does have scales but they are fairly far apart and mohair is therefore less likely to felt than wool. Although mohair has a delicate look, it is very strong and tough.

Many mohair yarns are sold as "brushed" yarns (figure 4-12). The long staple and strong fiber can readily stand up to the brushing process, although warp weaving yarns may be sold in an unbrushed, smooth state.

Mohair is a relatively expensive fiber and pure mohair yarn difficult to find. The yarn is sold mainly in mixtures with wool or as "mohair-type"

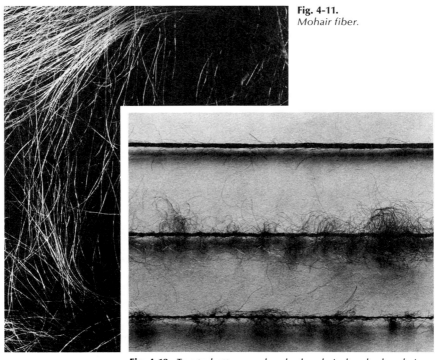

Fig. 4-11.
Mohair fiber.

Fig. 4-12. *Top to bottom: unbrushed mohair, brushed mohair, brushed "mohair-type" yarns.*

yarn, which may be mixed with synthetic as well as wool fibers. Pure mohair may be attacked by moths and mildew, although it is not as liable to this as wool. Some people find the long, spiky fibers quite irritating to the skin.

Rabbit Family
Rabbit fibers are particularly soft and silky.

Angora   The angora rabbit produces a fine, white, silky hair of roughly 1 to 3 inches (2 to 7.5 cm.) staple. The fiber is clipped every three or four months. Angora rabbits, like angora goats, were originally bred in Ankara (Turkey), but they are now extensively reared in France and in the U.S.

Grades of angora fiber are determined by color as well as staple length. Although all angora fiber is white, there are various grades of color categorized as pure white, white, lightly matted, and discolored. The fiber is especially soft and slippery, and has a silky sheen and feel. It can readily be dyed to a pastel shade   and is popular for its texture, warmth, light weight, and the delicate colors it is sold in. The fiber is too slippery to be readily spun on its own, and is, therefore, usually mixed with lamb's wool (figure 4-13).

Working with the slippery angora yarn is pleasant and easy. It shows up well in hand-knitting, and the attractive fluffy fabric is best preserved by shaking the whole garment or article after washing and allowing it to dry in a warm atmosphere. This procedure restores the full beauty of the yarn.

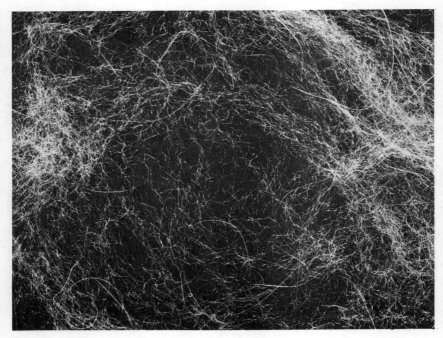

Fig. 4-13. *Angora and lamb's wool fibers; the long hairs are angora fibers.*

Rabbit The hair fibers from breeds of rabbits other than angora are also available. The staple is short by comparison, but the fibers retain the characteristic soft feel of rabbit's fur.

Linen

An excellent plant fiber comes form the stem of the flax plant (*Linum usitatissimum*), a slender annual with bright blue flowers. The yarn and fabrics made from flax are called linen and are known to have been used in ancient Egypt over six thousand years ago. Linen culture can be traced as far back as the Stone Age.

Although the plant grows easily, fiber extraction is involved, time-consuming, and labor intensive. Consequently, linen is now very expensive. The most famous linen-producing countries are Belgium, Ireland, and Scotland, and large quantities of the coarser linen yarns are also produced in the U.S.S.R. Flax is grown in the U.S. and Canada, but the plants are primarily for linseed production, and, as the seed has to be allowed to ripen for this purpose, the plant stems are past the fiber-producing stage when harvested. This is the reason that linen yarns marketed in the U.S. are all imported yarns.

Preparation of the Fiber

There are several methods of preparing and spinning flax fiber. These different methods affect the characteristics of the linen to a considerable extent, and linen yarn comes in a number of quite different qualities.

The plants are pulled from the soil, root and all. They are then stripped of leaves and seeds by a process called "rippling" (passing the stalks through coarse combs). The bundles of stripped stalks are then steeped in water, where they remain completely submerged for a period of five days to four weeks, depending on the method used. This process is called "retting." It allows the tissues around the flax fibers to decompose, leaving the fibers themselves available for further processing.

Methods of Retting

Different methods of retting produce different qualities of fiber. Stream retting produces the highest-quality fiber, particularly when done in slow-moving water with a low iron and lime content. Pool retting, the method used primarily in Ireland, makes use of stagnant pools of water for the process. Dew retting, in which the stalks lie on grass and are exposed to the elements for up to four weeks, produces strong, coarse fibers. It is the method favored in the U.S.S.R. Chemical and mechanical retting can also be used, shortening the retting time but producing less strong fiber.

Hackling

After retting, the partially decomposed tissue is separated from the flax fiber by several other operations. Eventually, the fibers are hackled (put through combs) one or more times so that short and broken fibers are combed out and the long flax fibers end up separated, smooth, and parallel to each other.

These long fibers are cut into three or four sections. The root and top ends, separated from the longer middle cuts, are known as "tow." The root ends contain coarse, short, low-quality fibers, and the tops, though of high quality, are of mixed length and thickness. The tow is processed into yarn much as cotton is spun into yarn (figure 4-14). Both high-and low-quality yarns are available.

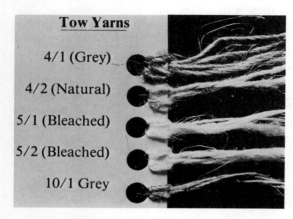

Tow Yarns

4/1 (Grey)

4/2 (Natural)

5/1 (Bleached)

5/2 (Bleached)

10/1 Grey

Fig. 4-14.
Linen tow yarns.

The middle fibers, separated by the cut after hackling, are the most valuable, as they are of even length and good quality. They give the type of flax fiber known as "line." Long line is fiber made of a complete middle cut; cut line is fiber made from a middle cut that is long enough to warrant cutting in two.

Line fibers have a staple length of between 12 and 20 inches (30 and 50 cm.) and are ready for spinning. These fibers are "wet-spun" (thoroughly wetted in hot water just before drafting) to produce finer, softer, more even yarns, though all linen yarns have a slightly "slubby" (thick and thin) appearance (figure 4-15).

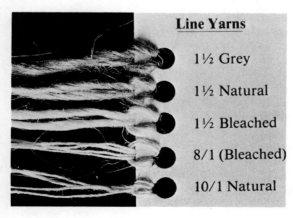

Line Yarns

1½ Grey

1½ Natural

1½ Bleached

8/1 (Bleached)

10/1 Natural

Fig. 4-15.
Linen line yarns.

The unit of measuring linen is generally called the "lea" ("cut" in Scotland) and measures 300 yards to the pound. The heavier yarns are sometimes measured by the spyndle (14,400 yards to the pound for dry-spun linen tow yarns) and referred to in terms of weight, so that "8 pound tow yarn" refers to a linen yarn count of 6 lea (see chapter 7). The average thickness of line yarn is 160 lea, but yarns spun to as fine as 400 lea may be used in Irish cambric or lawn. Linen has been spun to as fine as 760 lea, but only by hand and then only in the very damp atmosphere provided in special cellars. This size yarn is too fine to be seen by the naked eye, and the size it is spun to is controlled purely by feel. Such very fine yarn was traditionally used to make high-quality laces (figure 4-16).

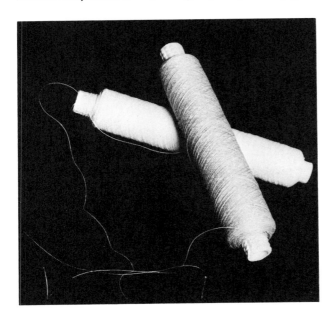

Fig. 4-16.
Modern linen lace yarn.

Color

Unbleached linen yarns are said to be "in the gray." Although such yarns are very strong, they are readily attacked by mildew. Most linen is, therefore, bleached in spite of the fact that this affects the strength of the yarn.

Three grades of bleached yarns are commonly offered: gray, natural, and bleached (see figures 4-14 and 4-15). The strength of the yarn varies with the bleaching. Highly colored linen must be fully bleached to absorb the dye properly. As with cotton, mercerization of linen helps to produce strong yarns with a good affinity to dyes. Yarns dyed to pastel shades do not pose any problems, but deep-dyed linen yarns need to be checked for adequate dye penetration; this is easily done by untwisting them. As you can see from figure 4-17, there are areas of undyed fiber even in a high-quality yarn.

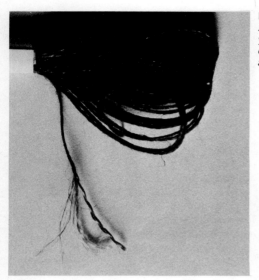

Fig. 4-17.
*A dark-colored linen
yarn shows that the
dye has not penetrated
all the fibers.*

Silk

Silk is a natural textile fiber produced by certain caterpillars. These caterpillars, called silkworms, envelop themselves in cocoons that protect them during their transformation from caterpillar to moth. The fibers the silkworms spin are very fine and consist of two strands (baves) that are extruded from the caterpillar's spinneret (gland for spinning). The baves are covered in sericin (silk gum), which makes up roughly 25 percent of the weight of the raw silk fiber. The mature caterpillar weaves hundreds of yards of this fiber round itself. Some of this fiber mass can be reeled out from the cocoon, provided the grub inside is killed at the right time in the cycle, and provided the cocoons are treated to soften the sericin. This sequence is the initial stage in the process of obtaining reeled raw silk fiber from which the highest-quality silk yarns are made. Broken silk filaments and silk waste of various kinds can be used in the form of spun silk, as explained below.

The first reference to silk is in China, circa 2600 B.C. The secret of silk manufacture was smuggled out of China three thousand years later and spread from Constantinople through Europe and eventually to America. Significant attempts at silk culture were made in Virginia in 1619, and in 1622 encouragement was given in the form of bounties and rewards offered to the colonists by James I of England. Benjamin Franklin, for instance, was engaged in sericulture (silk manufacture) in Philadelphia at the beginning of the War of Independence. After the war, a new effort to revive the industry never really caught on owing to the high labor costs. In spite of the fact that silk is primarily an imported fiber, the U.S. is still the largest importer and consumer of silk in the world.

Types of Silkworm

There are several different types of silkworm. Cultivated silk comes from moths of the *Bombycidae* family, the silkworms that feed on mulberry leaves. The best known of these is *Bombyx mori*. This silkworm prefers the leaf of the white-fruited mulberry (*Morus alba*) and produces the finest-quality raw silk fiber. Good cocoons can produce up to 1400 yards (1200 meters) of reeled silk filaments, varying in diameter from 1/1600 to 1/2500 inch. The filament thickness varies with the type of cocoon and the season at which it is reeled; some silkworms naturally have several life cycles in a year, others can be forced to do so artificially. The filaments are reeled from several cocoons at a time to produce even, raw silk yarns consisting of between four and twenty baves. The sericin binds the baves together and the raw silk is reeled into 450-meter lengths.

Wild silkworms (generally members of the *Antherea* and *Attacus* families) feed primarily on oak, castor oil, and cherry tree leaves. The filaments tend to be somewhat coarser in diameter than those produced under cultivation, varying between 1/600 and 1/1100 inch. Wild silk is less smooth than cultivated silk. The tannin in the oak leaves also tends to color the silk a gray-brown shade that is hard to bleach out. This silk is known as "tusser," "tussore," "tussah," or "tussor" silk, and it is often sold in its undyed state. Wild silk is fairly nubbly and the yarn has a slub appearance (figure 4-18).

Fig. 4-18. *A selection of wild silk yarns.*

Types of Silk Spinning

The reeled silk filaments can be used as they are or combined in several ways by being "thrown" into silk threads consisting of folded and cabled filament yarns (see chapter 7). The size of the thrown silk is based on a unit called the denier. The weight of the standard 450-meter length of the raw silk skein is defined as one denier if twenty such skeins weigh one gram. The average weight of raw silk is something like .7 gram for a single 450-meter skein. This is expressed as 14 denier or 13/15 denier to allow for small variations along the filament length (see chapter 7).

After the silk has been "thrown" into yarn, it is degummed (some or all of the sericin is removed). Some silk yarns are then weighted with metallic substances to replace the weight lost through degumming. Weighting is usually done at the dyeing stage, and the term *pure-dyed silk* indicates that such weights have not been added when the yarn was dyed.

Silk waste is made of various types of silk filaments. The filaments obtained from pierced cocoons, doubled cocoons, the first and last reelings of good cocoons, and machine waste left from reeled silk manufacture can all be sorted and graded into silk staple that can be spun on any of the usual staple spinning systems (figure 4-19). The cotton system is the one usually used, and the thickness of spun silk yarn is numbered with a cotton count number although the numbering is read in a different way. For example, "80/2 spun silk yarn" means that yarn has two strands of 160s cotton count number yarns combined to form an 80s yarn (see chapter 7).

Silk is the strongest natural fiber. It is reasonably elastic, has good resilience, is a nonconductor of heat, gives good drapability, and can be obtained with plenty of luster. Silk is not especially liable to attack by mildew or moths, and it has good affinity to dyes. At one time, pure silk yarns were very difficult to find, but now many suppliers are introducing a good range of silk or silk-blend yarns.

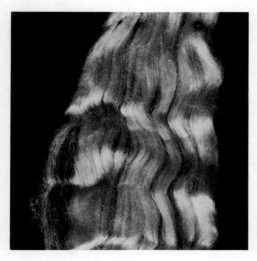

Fig. 4-19.
Silk sliver ready for spun-silk manufacture.

5/ Man-made Fibers: Acetate, Acrylic, Metallic, Nylon, Polyester, Rayon, and Triacetate

There are two types of man-made fibers: "regenerated" fibers, produced from naturally fibrous materials such as cotton linters or wood pulp; and "synthetic" fibers, made from materials consisting only of simple chemical elements, not in themselves in a fibrous form, such as tar, water, and petroleum products. Each man-made fiber belongs to a specific generic group, and the fiber groups discussed here are described under the generic group fiber name. Some man-made fibers are produced by cutting a very thin sheet of extruded fiber film into strips. These strips can be used as monofilament yarns, or several strips can be combined to make multifilament yarns (figure 5-1).

Most man-made textile fibers, however, are produced by forcing a viscous solution (melt) through holes in a device called a spinneret, as already discussed in chapter 1. The spinneret holes can be large or, more usually, very small. Their cross section may be circular, trilobal, hexagonal, or any other shape that gives good results.

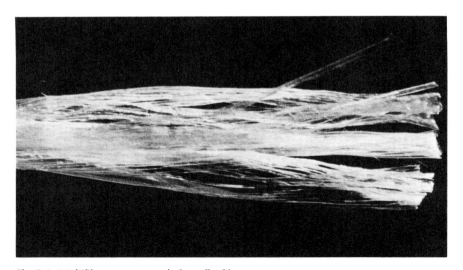

Fig. 5-1. *Multifilament yarn made from flat filaments.*

It is easy to see how fibers can be spun from viscous fluids. You have probably come across spun sugar produced from syrup made of sugar and water boiled together into a fairly thick syrup. The sugar threads or filaments are made by dipping a spoon or other implement into the warm syrup solution and spinning it (waving it rapidly) between two fixed objects. The spun liquid dries in the air into a very fine, solid thread.

The original substance that is to be made into a textile fiber may start out as a solid material, just like the sugar. The solid material has to be dissolved, melted, or chemically converted into some form of liquid that is then forced or extruded through the holes in the specially made spinneret. The continuous threads or filaments emerging from the spinneret are then solidified into textile fibers. The process is called spinning and is analogous to the spinning of a cocoon by the silkworm, or a web by the spider (see figure 5-2), and is quite different from the meaning of spinning associated with making a yarn from staple fibers. The filaments emerging from the spinneret are solidified (1) by passing the filaments through a chemical bath, in which case the process is called "wet spinning," (2) by passing the filaments through warm air, in which case the process is called "dry spinning," or (3) by passing the filaments through cooling air, in which case the process is called "melt spinning."

After the filaments have been produced, they may be stretched to introduce various new fiber characteristics. Such processes are used to strengthen or weaken characteristics inherent in the fiber solution. Viscose rayon, for example, can be made to have greater dry strength and less extensibility if the filaments are stretched after extrusion. However, the wet strength will then be lower.

Fig. 5-2. *Spiders' webs.*

Standard Measuring Units

The standard measuring units for the man-made fibers are derived from those used for the natural fibers in the past.

Filament Yarns

The standard units of measurement for the extruded filaments are the denier and the tex. The denier is the unit already discussed for reeled silk and is the weight, in grams, of 9,000 meters of filament. The more modern unit, the tex, designates the weight, in grams, of 1,000 meters of filament, so that 1 tex equals 9 denier. The larger the tex or denier number, the greater the cross-sectional width of the filament.

Spun Yarns

All man-made fibers are first produced in the form of continuous filaments: the actual length is determined by the convenience of a particular packaging unit for the manufacturer. However, these filaments can be turned into staples and this is often done in order to produce a yarn that more closely resembles yarns made from natural fibers.

A single spinneret may have up to 250,000 holes, and the tow (the rope of fibers) that emerges from the melt-, dry-, or wet-spinning processes can be cut into regular or irregular staple lengths. These staples can then be processed in the usual ways used for spinning natural staple fibers. Cutting the tow into staple and then spinning the staple involves the usual spinning operations. However, it is also possible to proceed directly from the tow to staple spinning. This can be done by cutting the tow into staple as the tow is processed, or by putting the tow under tension so that random breakage occurs along each of the filament lengths at the weakest points in the filaments. This type of procedure is called direct spinning and, as it can save some intermediate processes, is cheaper than the indirect staple spinning discussed above.

Staple man-made fibers can be spun on any of the conventional systems (see chapter 6). The unit of measurement used for such yarns is the unit adopted for natural yarns spun on that particular system. Therefore, if an acrylic staple fiber is spun on the worsted system, the unit of measurement for that yarn will be the worsted count (see chapter 7).

Bulked and Textured Filaments and Yarns

The man-made filaments or staples are fairly uniform and smooth and would not, as such, make entirely satisfactory yarns for those textile projects which are best worked with the fuzzy, softer yarns. The crimp or curl found in natural fiber yarns would be missing (figure 5-3), and various methods have been worked out to produce yarns that are more like the traditional yarns made from natural fibers. Although cutting the filaments into staples and then spinning these staples will make better yarns than simply using the filaments, even the staple yarns can be improved.

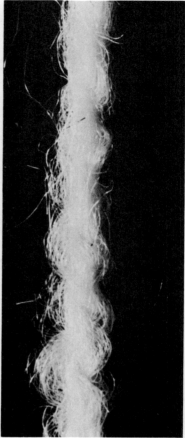

Fig. 5-3. *Soft-spun wool yarns showing the crimp in the wool fibers.*

Fig. 5-4. *Textured filament yarn; the magnification shows that the longer filaments are forced into a coiled shape.*

Textured Yarns

Special machinery can be used to manipulate each continuous filament in such a way that it is wavy along the length. The filaments can be modified by introducing coils, snarls, crinkles, or crimps. These modifications are very easily put into thermoplastic filaments or yarns while the yarn structure is heated and will become permanently set as the filament or yarn structure cools. Such texturing will improve moisture-holding capacity, resilience, elasticity, and handle of the yarn.

Bicomponent Yarns

Two different polymers can be extruded side by side to form a single fiber in much the same way that the silkworm extrudes two threads. If two such polymers have different sensitivities to heat or moisture and are then subjected to either heat or moisture during the finishing or dyeing processes, one of the components will react more strongly than the other. One strand will shrink, that is shorten in length, while the other remains unaffected. The unaffected filament will then be forced to spiral round the shortened filament in order to distribute its extra length. The fiber will now have much greater bulk, so that yarn made of it will have both greater covering power and greater warmth (figure 5-4).

High-bulk Yarns
Blends of low- and high-shrinkage potential staples can be spun together on any desired system. If the yarn made of them is then subjected to a high enough temperature to shrink some but not all of the fibers, a proportion of the fibers will become shorter, and the rest will retain their original length. The unaffected fibers will be forced to curl or bend in the yarn structure, and the yarn will have greater bulk and feel much warmer.

Cross-sectional Shapes
The cross-sectional shapes in which the filaments are extruded from the spinneret need not be circular. Different filament cross sections will entwine in different ways, and such differences can be useful in controlling the reflection of light. Synthetic yarns are often disliked because they are too shiny; if the cross section of the filaments is made octagonal, a glitter-free effect can be obtained. If, on the other hand, sparkle is a desirable characteristic, trilobal cross-sectional shapes will help provide it.

Special Additives
Various types of additives can be combined with the initial solutions before the filaments are extruded. Properties such as flame retardancy and anti-static can be added to the yarns.

Dye can also be added to the viscous substance to be extruded. "Solution" dyeing affords a very high degree of colorfastness in the fiber and eliminates the separate, costly process of dyeing the yarn.

Biconstituent Yarns
The substance to be extruded can be made of two different polymers (synthetic material from which fibers are formed) so that the characteristics from two materials can be combined in a single fiber.

Regenerated Fibers
The regenerated fibers are made by re-forming cellulose, which can be in the form of cotton linters, wood pulp, or any other substance containing an adequate amount of cellulose, into a liquid substance refined to pure cellulose and extruded, through a spinneret, into an acid bath to coagulate the fibers.

Wood chips, cotton linters, or other unrefined cellulose are treated with caustic soda in several processes, until it is finally transformed into a thick viscous solution called "viscose." After further purifying treatments, it is ready to be forced through the spinneret holes into a bath of sulfuric acid and then wet-spun into regenerated cellulose filaments.

Rayon

Rayon is a manufactured fiber composed of regenerated cellulose. Trade names include Beau-Grip, Coloray, Encron, Fibro, Xena, and Zantrel.

Rayon was the first man-made fiber. Although the idea of creating a man-made textile fiber is known to have been thought about in ancient China, the first rayon was not produced until the nineteenth century. It was not until 1925, however, that the Federal Trade Commission permitted the use of the name *rayon* for yarns made from cellulose or its derivatives. Even then, the different types of rayon on the market caused confusion, and in 1952 the Federal Trade Commission ruled that there would be two categories of fibers made of cellulose, to be called "rayon" and "acetate" (defined below). Although it was clear that rayon was a man-made fiber, it also became clear that it was different from the "synthetic" fibers which, although also man-made, were not made from natural, cellulosic materials but from chemical elements. Rayon is therefore called a "regenerated" fiber.

At first the fiber was known as "artificial silk" because it resembled the look, though not necessarily the properties, of silk fibers. Rayon is not really like silk although some shiny rayons do have the look of silk (figure 5-5). Rayon fiber properties are very different from those of silk fiber.

Viscose Rayon   The "standard" rayon, called "viscose" or "viscose rayon" is usually made of wood pulp obtained from softwood trees such as pine or spruce. The fiber is initially produced in filament form but can be cut to staple and spun on the cotton or woolen systems. Both conventional spinning and direct spinning are used to make the staple yarns. Viscose rayon is one of the most absorbent of all textile fibers, as well as being a good conductor of heat so that it is an excellent fiber for summer wear. Dyes are evenly absorbed and the crimped staple, made by forming a thicker skin down one side of the filament during production, gives increased resilience and warmth. The specific gravity of rayon is quite high so that fabrics made with this fiber have good drapability. Moths do not attack cellulosic fibers.

Although elasticity in rayon is greater than that in cotton or in linen, it does not compare with that of wool or silk. Viscose rayon is a weak fiber, weaker still in the wet state, and care is needed when laundering. Shrinkage can be a problem if the fiber has not been treated with a shrink-resistant finish. Mildew will form readily if the yarn or fabric made of viscose is left in a damp state.

Viscose rayon can be purchased as a high-luster yarn which can be very attractive on its own. It can also be used to add interest when the yarn is combined with a mat yarn. However, the high-luster yarns are very slippery and precautions may have to be taken to prevent the yarn from tangling when it is being used. The foot from an old nylon stocking or panty hose

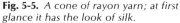

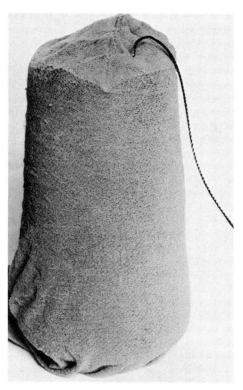

Fig. 5-5. *A cone of rayon yarn; at first glance it has the look of silk.*

Fig. 5-6. *An end of rayon yarn threaded through the foot of a nylon stocking helps prevent the yarn from tangling in use.*

slipped over the yarn package, with a yarn end threaded through, will overcome this problem (figure 5-6).

Several processes can be carried out on the rayon filaments to give them added properties. For instance, high wet modulus rayon can be produced by stretching the fibers after coagulation, adding greater water absorption to the fibers and also increasing their wet strength.

Cuprammonium Rayon Cuprammonium rayon differs from viscose rayon in that the purified cellulose is mixed with copper sulfate and ammonia (the word *cuprammonium* is a combination of these two words). The solution is then extruded through the spinneret, and, after the fiber emerges, it is treated to remove the copper and ammonia and immersed in a bath of sulfuric acid in which it is stretched as it coagulates. This "stretch spinning" produces a very fine filament which can be turned into yarn with a particularly soft feel and a subdued luster.

The other properties of cuprammonium rayon are much the same as those of viscose.

Acetate

Acetate is a manufactured fiber in which the fiber-forming substance is cellulose acetate. The term *triacetate* may be used as a generic description for a more than 92 percent degree of acetylation (combining cellulose with acetic acid). Trade names include Ariloft, Celanese, and Chromspun.

Rayon is produced by converting natural cellulose into a filament; acetate and triacetate begin with the pure cellulose produced from the same raw materials as rayon, but these are then mixed with sulfuric and other acids into a viscous fluid. The final, extruded filament is a chemical derivative of cellulose called an "ester." Because the acetate fibers are *modified* cellulosic fibers their properties are different from those of the purely cellulosic fibers.

Acetate fibers are more elastic than other rayons but still not very elastic. Acetate is fairly resilient, however, and fabrics made of it will not sag as much as other rayons. The drape is good, and acetate dries quickly and washes easily. It is resistant to mildew and moths, and it is warmer than other rayons.

Acetate cannot take much hard wear, however, and is even weaker than the other rayons. It tends to feel clammy in humid weather, as it is not very absorbent, and loses strength when wet, so care is needed in laundering. Acetate is also heat sensitive so that fabrics should be ironed at low temperatures.

Triacetate possesses all the properties of acetate but is also less water absorbent and more crease resistant. Triacetate is a thermoplastic fiber and, therefore, can have durable pleating set into fabric made of it.

Synthetic Fibers

The synthetic fibers are made from chemical elements combined in different ways. Staple fibers with distinct properties useful for domestic textile crafting can be produced, and the synthetics in most common use are discussed below.

All synthetics are immune to shrinkage caused by friction or immersion in water, but they are *not* immune to shrinkage caused by heat. However, many of the fibers are stabilized by heat-setting (see chapter 2); provided the heat used for the setting is not exceeded, the fibers will stay stable in the set structure so that they are, in effect, shrinkproof.

Acrylic

Basically, acrylic is a plastic made of petroleum derivatives. There are many differences in the acrylic group of chemically related fibers, but they share general characteristics. Trade names include Acrilan, Courtelle, Creslan, Dralon, Orlon, and Zefran.

Spun Yarn Acrylic fibers are wet-spun filaments measuring up to 10 denier. Most acrylic yarn is spun from staple fibers made by cutting the tow which emerges from the spinneret into 1½- to 5-inch lengths (3 to 7.5 cm.).

The staples are spun on the cotton or wool systems to produce fuzzy yarns with a soft feel. The yarns can have a low or high twist (see chapter 6). Low-twist yarns can be very soft to the touch—almost as soft as cashmere. Unfortunately, however, acrylics have a tendency to pill, and harder spun yarns show less of this tendency.

High-bulk Yarns   Acrylic fibers can have high or low shrinkage potential. If an acrylic yarn is made of a blend of high and low shrinkage potential fibers and subjected to a high temperature during the dyeing process, a proportion of the fibers will shrink and the rest will become highly crimped in the yarn structure. Such "high-bulk" yarn gives increased covering power and warmth. High-bulk acrylics are very popular and give excellent results when used for textile crafts. The size of the yarn, given in a count number, relates to the yarn *before* it is dyed. The yarn will therefore be shorter than the count number would suggest.

Abrasion resistance of acrylics is fairly good and compares favorably with wool. Acrylic is not a strong fiber, though it is stronger than wool. The fiber is reasonably resilient, and, as it is a poor conductor of heat, it can feel quite warm. High-bulk acrylics can have greater insulating power than wool for less weight. As the fiber has a strong tendency to pill and to become fuzzy, care is needed in laundering. Drying is quite slow, though not as slow as the drying of wool. Static electricity can be a problem with acrylics.

Metallic Fibers

Metallic fiber is a manufactured fiber made of metal, plastic-coated metal, metal-coated plastic, or a core yarn covered by metal. Brand names include Lurex, Lamé, and Metlon.

Metallic yarns and threads offer one of the most rewarding raw materials for textile crafts. Thin threads of metallic yarn, woven or knitted into a fabric, will give a touch of luxury to the plainest textile techniques. Metallic threads were the earliest man-made fibers. They were used in ancient civilizations in the Far East to weave beautiful patterns into clothing. The metals used were gold, silver, copper, and others which could be drawn out into very fine strands. Such strands are generally called "tinsel." The disadvantage of these threads was that, with the exception of gold, they tarnished when exposed to the air and they tended to cut into the other fibers they were woven in with. Tinsels also do not mold or drape well and are hard to clean. It is still possible to buy them, but it is important to make sure that only "tarnish-free" yarn is bought.

Modern metallic yarns are most often made by sandwiching a sheet of thin aluminum foil between two very thin layers of a clear plastic adhesive. These three layers, cut into very fine, flat, ribbonlike filaments, will produce a silver yarn unless some coloring matter is added to the plastic before it is bonded to the aluminum; opaque pigments can be added to reduce glitter. The laminated material is slit into whatever filament width is required, usually between 1/8 and 1/120 inch (figure 5-7).

The outstanding feature of metallic yarns is, of course, their sparkle and brilliance. The yarns will not tarnish or dull, as aluminum does not tarnish. Flexibility is ensured by the plastic covering (figure 5-8).

The strength of the metallic yarn depends on the type of plastic used. Many of these yarns can be used on their own for the weft in weaving, for hand-knitting, and for crochet. If the yarn appears too weak for warp yarn or for machine-knitting, greater strength can be added by combining it with "invisible" nylon monofilament (figure 5-9). The laundering temperatures depend on the type of plastic used for the yarn covering. All the fibers will be moth and mildew proof. Although metallics generally are inelastic, it is possible to buy a metallic yarn wrapped around a rubber core (figure 5-10).

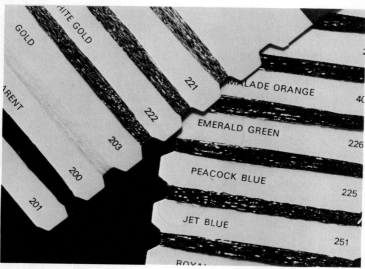

Fig. 5-7. *A range of colors for metallic yarns.*

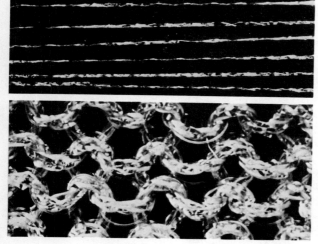

Fig. 5-8.
A twisted metallic filament yarn.

Fig. 5-9.
The magnification shows strength added to a weak metallic yarn by knitting an invisible nylon in with it.

Fig. 5-10. *Top to bottom: flat metallic filament yarn; metallic spun yarn; elastic metallic yarn.*

Nylon

Nylon fiber is a manufactured fiber produced from synthetic polyamides (basic fiber-forming substances).

Of the several types of nylon, the best-known are nylon 66 and nylon 6. Trade names include Antron, Beaunit Nylon, Cantrece, Elura, Qiana, and Ultron.

Nylon was developed by E. I. du Pont de Nemours and Co., which allowed W. H. Carothers, an organic chemist from Harvard, to undertake fundamental research in their laboratories. The company made it possible for Carothers to have his colleagues work on sidelines to his own immediate interests. One of these co-workers produced a polyamide solution, which he squirted into the air from a hypodermic syringe. The solution cooled into a fine filament and this was stretched into an even finer filament. The result was considered to be lustrous, strong, and flexible enough to show real promise as a textile fiber. Research into polyamide solutions continued until eventually two chemical compounds containing six carbon atoms per molecule were considered to be the best melt (viscous solution). This mixture was called the "6,6" polymer because each component contained six carbon molecules. The generic name *nylon* was adopted because it was a simple word; "nylon 6,6" or "nylon 66" was the first commercial nylon. Several other polyamides were also investigated: the second most popular nylon is "nylon 6" which is primarily made outside the U.S.

The main advantages of nylon are its tensile strength and excellent abrasion resistance. Nylon is also an elastic fiber and, being thermoplastic, is usually made shrink resistant by proper heat setting. Nylon can be produced in staple form from the initial filament in the same way as other man-made fibers.

Nylon fibers do not absorb much moisture; fabrics made of them tend to be uncomfortable in humid conditions even when made of "crimped" filament or staple. There is also a definite tendency to pilling, so that care is needed when laundering pure nylon fabrics in spite of the tensile strength of the fiber. Most nylons have a low melting point, and it is important to set ironing temperatures correctly. The monofilament yarns, used for sewing, machine knitting, and doubling with other yarns, can now be obtained with a reasonably high melting point so that fabrics sewn or strengthened with them can be ironed at sufficiently high temperatures (figure 5-11).

Most yarns for textile crafts are not made of pure nylon; the fiber is combined with a variety of others to make yarns with properties that modify the harsh handle, the tendency to static, the poor drape, and the low melting point of nylon. The tensile strength can, in fact, be too great. Knitting by machine with pure nylon yarn can cause problems should the yarn get caught in the machine mechanism, for instance. The yarn is so strong that parts of the machine may be bent out of shape; a weaker yarn would break before this could happen.

Nylon is particularly useful as part of a blended yarn. The percentage of nylon in the mixture is important, and yarn package labels will state precisely what that is. Although the inclusion of nylon will appreciably increase the desirable properties of the blend over its unblended counterpart, there is no necessary direct comparison, as already discussed in chapter 1. It is common to see the heels and toes of nylon/wool or nylon/cotton blend socks worn bare of the wool or cotton with only the nylon remaining (figure 5-12). Although this is not pretty, it does illustrate just how useful nylon can be.

Fig. 5-11.
Transparent or invisible nylon for dark and light yarns or fabrics.

Fig. 5-12.
Part of a sock made of nylon/cotton yarn; the cotton has worn away, leaving a grid of nylon.

Polyester

Polyester fiber is manufactured from synthetic polymer fiber-forming substances. There are several variations in the composition and consequently in the properties of polyester fiber. Trade names include Avlin, Blue "C," Encron, Fortrel, Kodel, Dacron, and Trevira.

W. H. Carothers intended to study the polyesters, but he was sidetracked by the more immediate promise of the polyamides and the discovery of nylon, thus allowing other scientists to take up the research into the polyesters. In particular, chemists of the Calico Printers' Association (U.K.) investigated polyesters with potential for textile fibers. The brand name "Terylene" was given to a successful fiber substance. Terylene is chemically similar to the "Dacron" polyester fiber now produced by the du Pont Company of the U.S.

The properties of polyester are similar to those of nylon. The fibers are very strong, though not quite as strong as nylon. Abrasion resistance of the fibers is good, but polyester is inferior to nylon for elasticity. Moisture absorption is low, lower even than nylon, so that fabrics made of Dacron, say, will dry very rapidly and will not stain easily because most of the moisture remains on the surface of the yarn or the fabric made of it. Polyester has the disadvantages of feeling clammy in humid weather conditions and of acquiring relatively high static electricity in dry weather conditions. Consequently, polyester fibers are frequently blended with cotton to offset these disadvantages. One of the big advantages of polyester yarns is that they do not stretch out of shape easily, so that garments made of them do not sag.

Polyester is a thermoplastic fiber and can be heat-set. If these fibers are not heat-set, they can be very troublesome because creases will be "set" by hot domestic laundering.

6/ Spinning: How Yarn Is Put Together from Staple Fibers

Although staple textile fibers cling to each other, they cannot form a sufficiently strong yarn structure unless they are spun. Spinning in this sense means drafting (drawing out) and twisting prepared staple fibers in such a way that a strand of yarn both strong and long enough to form a "single" or "singles" yarn is produced.

Some man-made fibers, as already discussed, are continuously processed (directly staple-spun from tow). This direct spinning method avoids several of the processes, such as sorting and carding the staples (aligning fibers, see below), preparatory to the spinning operation. The great majority of staple fibers, however, do need to be processed in several ways to prepare them for spinning. This applies to all the natural staple fibers, to silk waste, and to man-made filament fibers cut into staple from tow after it has been extruded.

Staple fibers are collected together in different types of packages, such as cotton fibers that arrive as bales from the cotton fields, wool fibers that arrive in rolled fleeces from the sheep farms (figure 6-1), or flax fibers that arrive as tow. These staple fiber masses have to be sorted, cleaned, and prepared for the twisting that finally produces a yarn structure strong enough to withstand the various textile processes which eventually turn yarn into fabric.

It is important to know something of the methods of yarn manufacture because that is the only way in which you can properly judge the yarns for yourself. You may still not know precisely how each yarn mill processes its raw fibers, but you can know the general principles of how yarns are put together, and this knowledge will substantially help you choose the correct yarn for the textile project you have in mind. This understanding of the general principles will enable you to choose a "weaving" yarn for some knitting projects, a "crochet" yarn for some lacemaking, or any substitute yarn of *your* choice to replace the particular yarn suggested in a pattern. The many different facets of yarn manufacture make yarn substitution difficult if you know little about yarns, and it is often suggested that only the yarn recommended in a pattern should be used in a particular textile project. However, in order to make original textiles, it is *your*, possibly idiosyncratic, choice of yarn which affords the first step in the creative process of making *your* fabric; you may well not wish to leave this choice to others.

Fig. 6-1.
A rolled fleece.

Preparatory Processes for Spinning

The raw fiber packages that are delivered to the yarn mills are first opened and examined (figure 6-2). Impurities, such as leaves or seeds in cotton fiber bales and burrs or dirt in wool fleeces, are removed. The method used depends on the state of the fiber, the fiber type, and the machinery available at the mill, but the end result is a fiber mass that is reasonably free from any foreign matter and is scoured (cleaned) and ready for further processing (figure 6-3).

Fig. 6-2. *The fleece contains impurities such as dried grass, dirt, and burs.*

Fig. 6-3. *Cleaned flax fibers.*

The fibers are now "carded." Carding is the disentanglement of fibers by passing them between two moving surfaces set with wire teeth or small spikes. Figure 6-4 shows a pair of hand carders. The word *carder* is derived from the medieval *carda*: to tease or comb. Originally a plant called a "teasel" (figure 6-5) was used for this purpose; the seed heads were crammed into box shapes and used to tease or card the fibers into thin sheets of aligned fibers called a web. Figure 6-6 shows some locks of Wensleydale wool and the same wool after carding. This process is now, of course, carried out on machinery.

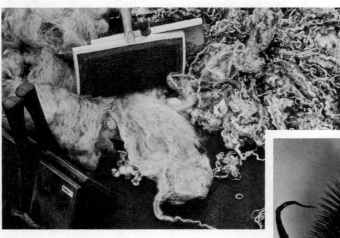

Fig. 6-4. *Two pairs of hand carders; one pair is shown turned inside out to show the metal spikes used to disentangle the fibers.*

Fig. 6-5. *The seed-head of a teasel flower, showing its spikes.*

Fig. 6-6. *Left: carded Wensleydale wool. Right: uncarded wool.*

At this stage two main types of preparation for spinning need to be distinguished. Cotton yarn is said to be carded or combed, and wool yarn is said to be "woolen-spun" or "worsted-spun" to distinguish the two ways of preparing the fibers before the actual spinning process. The terms *woolen-spun* and *worsted-spun* are also applied to fibers other than wool that have nonetheless been prepared in one or other of these ways.

Carded or Woolen-spun Yarn

The fibers in the card web will lie roughly parallel in a thin sheet. Most of the fibers used will be relatively short-stapled, that is, the staple length will be between 1 and 4 inches (2.5 and 10 cm.), depending on the fiber type. The web is now rolled to form a "rolag" so that the fibers lie more or less perpendicular to the length of the rolag, or two or more webs are placed on top of each other and rolled or funneled to form "card sliver," and then "roving." The rolag, sliver, or roving will all have many fibers lying perpendicular as well as parallel to the longitudinal axis of the fiber roll. These rolls are then drafted (drawn out) and twist is inserted into them. This is the actual spinning.

Combed or Worsted-spun Yarn

The sheep originally reared in the southeastern part of England (East Anglia) tended to have long-stapled fleeces with fiber lengths ranging from 4 to 10 inches (10 to 25 cm.). The spinning carried out in the area, and in particular near the town of Worstead (Worsted), produced lustrous, strong yarns. Consequently, the term *worsted* began to be used to describe a particular form of spinning as well as a type of yarn or a material made from worsted yarn.

The difference between spinning long-stapled fibers and short-stapled fibers is not only one of fiber length; the process also differs in that the long-stapled fibers are combed. This was originally done by using tools called "woolcombs" that looked something like very large metal combs and weighed between 5 and 8 pounds (2 and 3.5 kg.) each. The process is easily understood in terms of combing hair; the fibers are straightened out and made to lie parallel, and any short, broken, or unsuitable fibers are held back in the comb and discarded.

In the modern textile industry, worsted yarns are first carded and then combed, that is, an additional process is applied to the carded fibers. They are straightened and positioned parallel to each other by passing a comb through them or by subjecting them to several combings. The word used for combing, when applied to textile fibers, may vary with the fiber type: *hackling,* for instance, is the name used for parallellizing flax fibers. But, whatever the technical word used, the additional process or processes result in a much smoother web or comb sliver that has had the "noils" (short, broken, or other imperfect fibers) removed. The comb sliver can now be rolled or funneled into "tops" which will be ready for spinning (figure 6-7).

To sum up, there are two important classes of staple-spun yarns. The first, called carded or woolen-spun yarn, is made by spinning the rolled or

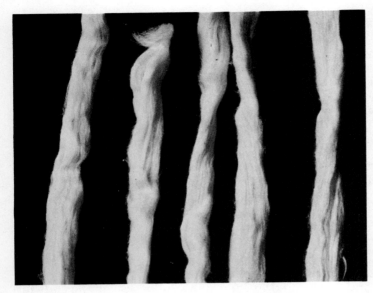

Fig. 6-7.
Worsted tops.

funneled card sliver produced after the original carding. The fibers used will be short-stapled and will lie at various angles to the longitudinal axis of the sliver.

The second, called combed or worsted-spun yarn, is made by spinning the tops produced from the comb sliver. The discarded noils may be of good quality and are often used for spinning yarn on the woolen system.

Three well-known systems of worsted spinning are the following:

American-spun Yarn American-spun yarn is produced on cotton yarn processing equipment. The fiber is processed in only five steps—a relatively short method of processing worsted yarn made from either natural or synthetic fiber. Prepared, untwisted top is used together with a small amount of antistatic oil. The yarns are spun from fibers averaging 3 inches (7.5 cm.) in length and given a medium twist.

Bradford-spun Yarn The Bradford (or English) system of worsted yarn spinning can handle longer fibers than the American or French system—up to 8 inches long (20 cm.). However, up to nine different processes are required to complete the yarn. Such yarns are often called "oil-spun" because oil is applied to the card sliver before combing. The yarns are strong and soft with a fairly high twist.

French-spun Yarn The French system of worsted spinning uses seven different processes. This system can make use of very short fibers—as short as 1¼ inches (3 cm.). French-spun yarns are "dry-spun," that is, oil is only applied to the card sliver in minute quantities to prevent the forming of static during the processing. The yarns are lofty and soft to handle as they are very softly spun.

Differences between Woolen and Worsted Yarns

The main differences between woolen and worsted yarns can be summarized as follows:

Woolen Yarn

Woolen yarns are primarily made from the shorter staple fibers, or from the shorter, possibly broken, noils discarded in the combing of the longer staples. Therefore, woolen yarns may be less expensive than worsted yarns because they may have been made from reprocessed raw material and require fewer processes to finish the yarn.

An important feature of woolen yarns is that the fibers lie at different angles to the longitudinal axis of the yarn (figure 6-8). This means that there are a great many air pockets within the yarn so that the construction is lofty and therefore feels warmer than an equivalent worsted-spun yarn with its parallel-packed fibers. Because one of the purposes of spinning on the woolen system is to preserve as much air in the yarn as possible, woolen yarns generally have only a soft twist inserted. The yarn will also be whiskery, with fibers protruding along the length.

Woolen-spun yarns will be weaker, bulkier, and softer than worsteds, giving better cover and more warmth. Abrasion resistance will not be as good as for the worsteds, but the general feel will be light, fluffy, and altogether more suitable for some uses than worsteds.

Worsted Yarns

Worsted yarns are made from the longer staple fibers (figure 6-9). Such yarns are often, though by no means always, made of the more expensive fibers. Worsteds have to be combed as well as carded, an extra process that

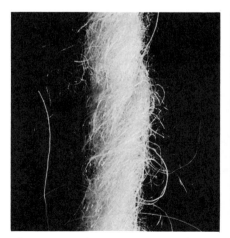 

Fig. 6-8. *A woolen-spun yarn. Note the lofty structure of the yarn, and the way fibers lie at various angles to the longitudinal axis of the yarn.*

Fig. 6-9. *A worsted-spun yarn. Note the smooth structure of the yarn, and the way the fibers lie parallel to the longitudinal axis of the yarn.*

Fig. 6-10.
The use of worsted or combed cotton yarns ensures clear lines in the tapestry weaving.

inevitably adds to the cost of the yarn. These additional costs are compensated for by producing a lustrous, smooth, strong, and long-lasting yarn, with a delightful clarity of line which can be used to show fabric pattern to great advantage (figure 6-10). Worsteds can also be used to reflect light in different directions in a fabric.

Amount of Twist

After the fibers have been processed into roving or tops, they will need to be drafted and spun. This means that the amount of fiber needed for a particular yarn thickness will have to be drawn out of the prepared fiber roll and the amount of twist needed to stop the fibers from slipping past each other will have to be applied.

Figure 6-11 shows that it is easy to separate out the individual fibers from an unspun fiber mass. Figure 6-12 shows some worsted tops: the fibers are still easy to separate from each other, simply by pulling the fibers sideways. Figure 6-13 shows a "sheep's coat" singles yarn. Clearly the fibers will not pull away from each other nearly as easily; the fiber surfaces will interlock and curl around each other so that the strength needed to pull the fibers apart will increase substantially over that needed to pull an untwisted fiber mass apart. Figure 6-14 shows a yarn which has been "spun" in the conventional textile sense of the word.

Fig. 6-11.
An unspun mass of Herdwick fibers.

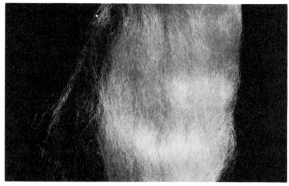

Fig. 6-12.
Worsted tops; the fibers are still easy to separate from the fiber mass.

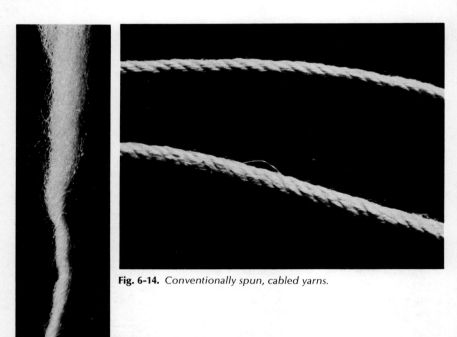

Fig. 6-14. *Conventionally spun, cabled yarns.*

Fig. 6-13.
*A singles slub yarn, alternating
soft- and very soft-spun portions.*

Although spinning imparts twist, there is a choice in the *amount* of twist a particular yarn is subjected to. This amount is given in TPI (twists per inch) or TPC (twists per centimeter), and the look of the yarn, its strength, and the end use to which it will be put are all substantially affected by the amount of twist used in the spinning.

The fiber mass will start out soft and fluffy. As soon as a certain amount of twist is inserted, the mass will become much more dense and compact, and, though still reasonably fluffy, will have a more "yarnlike" look. After the twist is increased, the softness will gradually be replaced by a compact, thready appearance, and, if the twist is increased a good deal, the yarn will eventually snarl back on itself. You can prove all this quite easily by twisting a piece of softly spun knitting yarn in several stages.

As a worsted-spun yarn is twisted, the fibers move from their position parallel to the longitudinal axis of the yarn to one which is at an angle to this yarn axis. This position is measured in angles and the greater the angle to the yarn axis, the more tightly spun is the yarn. Generally, angles of twist start from as low as 5° for very soft-spun yarn, to angles of 45° which give a very hard twist. The various grades between range from soft, to medium, to hard.

The number of turns per inch *can* be a useful guide to the amount of twist in a yarn, but the number of turns needed to produce a soft or hard twist will vary with the thickness of the yarn. Clearly a fairly bulky yarn will need less twist in it to hold the fibers together than a very thin one, because the fiber mass will already afford some strength just by being a relatively large mass in a yarn shape. For this reason, some bulky yarns can be sold as little more than roving (figure 6-15). Such yarns are strong enough to withstand the rigors of hand-knitting, but they would not be strong enough to use on a knitting machine.

As far as weaving yarns are concerned, the warps will have to be much stronger than the wefts (see chapter 8). Very soft-twisted yarns, therefore, are completely unsuitable as warps and may even be too soft to withstand the beating-in applied to wefts. Nevertheless, very *bulky* yarns, however softly spun, may well be suitable as "effect" weft yarns in parts of a woven fabric (figure 6-16).

At the other end of the scale are the very hard-twist yarns. These are twisted just to the point where they would turn back on themselves if twisted farther. They wear well and give a smooth look to fabric made of them.

Fig. 6-15.
Wool roving.

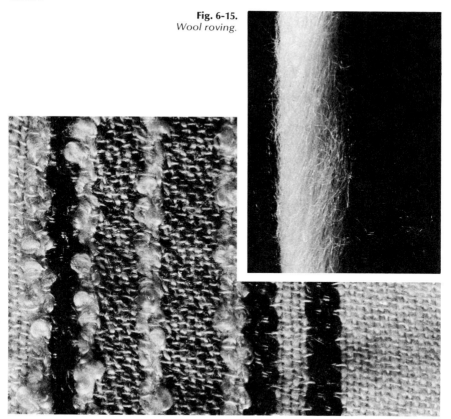

Fig. 6-16. *Soft-spun "effect" yarns in a woven fabric.*

Direction of Twist

The twisting of yarn can be done in two ways: clockwise and counter-clockwise. At first it would seem that the direction is not important and that it depends on the machinery available. The machinery does, of course, affect which way a mill will twist its yarns, but the introduction of that machinery in the first place will have had a reason. The two different twists are best distinguished from each other by looking at yarn, held perpendicularly, relative to its axis. Figure 6-17 shows S-twist and Z-twist yarns, so called because the letters *S* and *Z* have opposite middle sections which easily remind one of the direction the yarn is twisted in. Both twists have their special uses, and it is the *combination* of yarns of different twists which often leads to exciting light-reflecting patterns in woven fabrics.

Singles are spun as S-twists or Z-twists. Although the directions can be used to make patterns in woven fabric, the direction itself is not critical for weaving. There is, however, a very important difference between S-twist and Z-twist yarns as far as knitting and crochet are concerned. Knitting with yarn threaded through the right-hand fingers is generally thrown (wrapped round the needle) in a counterclockwise direction in the U.S. and U.K. In some Eastern countries the preferred direction is clockwise. The important result from the point of view of U.S. and U.K. knitters is that a Z-twist yarn will *untwist* if knitted in the usual way. Z-twist singles, therefore, have disadvantages for hand-knitting, particularly if they are very soft-twisted. The fibers will untwist and the knitting needle may catch in the fiber mass. On the other hand, a hard-spun singles that will not unwind enough to cause split-yarn or split-fiber problems may cause a different sort of problem. The fabric may become distorted by the twist, forming a lopsided, bias fabric.

Fig. 6-17.
Z-twist and S-twist singles.

Crochet yarns are generally threaded through the fingers of the left hand, and the normal crocheting action used by right-handed people tightens a Z-twist yarn and slackens an S-twist yarn. Crocheting is therefore perfectly feasible for a soft-spun Z-twist yarn. A hard-spun yarn, on the other hand, has the same disadvantages for crocheting as for knitting: the fabric may distort in the direction of the twist.

Folded Yarns

Singles are relatively easy and inexpensive to produce, but they have certain disadvantages. They may lack strength, they may untwist during crafting, and they may cause knitted or crocheted fabric made of them to be formed on the bias.

It is not hard to guess that some of these disadvantages might be overcome by combining several singles. Indeed, a very highly twisted singles yarn may twist back on itself to form a naturally "doubled up" yarn. Figure 6-18 shows that the "doubled" part of the yarn is twisted in the opposite direction to the original singles yarn. This suggests that combining several singles, perhaps in the opposite twist direction to the one they were spun in, might be useful. Two or more strands wound round each other would be stronger than a singles of the same width, any unevennesses in the original singles would have a good chance of canceling out, and the yarn would be a "balanced" one—that is, the yarn structure would be in equilibrium (figure 6-19).

Singles can be "folded" (combined) in several ways. Assuming that the original singles were all spun as S-twists and then combined with a Z-twist, we could abbreviate this to SZ, the first letter referring to the twist in the singles, the second to the twist of the fold. Obviously, yarns can also be folded ZS, SS, and ZZ. The first two categories are generally described as "plied" yarns, the second as "twist-on-twist" yarns. All crafters will be familiar with plied yarns. Folding singles in the opposite twist direction will reduce their original amount of twist and, therefore, make them softer, but the added strength and balance obtained from the process will more than make up for this. The act of plying yarns is particularly valuable for hand-knitting, as this technique involves looping yarn around a needle, so the yarn has to be very flexible yet reasonably strong. Plied yarns are excellent for this purpose. Twist-on-twist yarns are generally too stiff for ordinary hand-knitting. Most hand-knitting yarns are ZS, for reasons already discussed above, and they are generally available as 2-ply, 3-ply, and 4-ply yarns. The *thickness* of the separate strands making up the plied yarns is not specified in such terms and will be discussed in chapter 7, but the *number* of strands is given by the ply, sometimes called the "fold," number (figure 6-20).

Weaving yarns are often singles, but folded yarns are also used, particularly for warp yarns. Folded yarns add strength, luster, and texture to woven fabrics. Worsted weaving yarns are best plied to retain their luster: twist-on-twist yarns will have yarn fibers almost perpendicular to the yarn axis and will appear less lustrous.

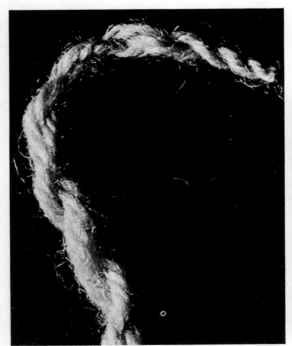

Fig. 6-18.
A plied yarn twisted to fold back on itself: note that the direction of the twist is opposite to the original twist direction.

Fig. 6-19. *A "balanced" yarn.*

Fig. 6-20. *4-ply yarns; note that, although the yarns are all offered on the same sample card, their thicknesses vary.*

Doubled Yarns

It is quite possible to use several yarn strands together without inserting any twist into them. This is called doubling the yarn, whatever the number of ends used. Many embroidery yarns are made in this way (figure 6-21), but it is also possible to design your own doubled yarns for weaving or knitting. Doubled weaving yarns can be very effective; however, hand-knitting with doubled yarns has certain drawbacks, as with loosely twisted singles, but this method of combining yarns to their own design is much favored by machine-knitters.

Fig. 6-21. *A stranded embroidery yarn; six 2-ply yarns are doubled together.*

Cabled Yarns

Folded yarns can be combined with each other to form "cabled" yarns. Again, the balanced SZS and ZSZ ("cable") twists are often preferred to the SSZ or ZZS ("hawser") twists, although the latter are also used. The first letter refers to the singles twist, the second to the folding twist, and the third to the cabling twist.

Cabled yarns, sometimes called "corded" yarns, tend to form a much rounder yarn, even stronger than the folded yarns (figure 6-22).

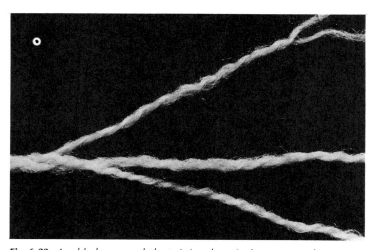

Fig. 6-22. *A cabled yarn made by twisting three 2-ply yarns together.*

Novelty or Fancy Yarns

Although spinning is essential for a reasonably strong, even, and uniform yarn, the process can also be used to add textural effects of various kinds to singles, folded, or cabled yarns. Colors, thicknesses, fibers, and S- or Z-twistings at regular or random intervals can be inserted in the yarns. Although novelty yarns are generally not as strong or as hard-wearing as conventionally spun yarns, they are useful for producing unusual fabrics while using only the simplest craft techniques.

The construction of conventional singles and folded yarns is intended to achieve the greatest uniformity possible in the yarn. Cabling the yarns increases this uniformity still further, and almost completely round, very strong yarns can be made in this way. It is, however, possible to use the spinning process to make yarns with carefully controlled irregularities (figure 6-23) such as added nubs (lumps), coils, or loops in the singles. Or, the yarns can be folded in such a way that one is delivered faster than another and yarns of different thicknesses, colors, or effects are put together. "Effect" yarns are yarns which differ sufficiently from the main yarn in terms of fiber, thickness, or construction to stand out in a fabric pattern.

Novelty yarns can be produced by many methods and suppliers provide a good range. These yarns can add interest and pattern to fabrics made of them, provided common sense is used to avoid complications—for example, embroidering with a bouclé yarn would be tiresome as the nubs might well be too large to slip through the material being embroidered. Also, novelty yarns are generally not as durable as yarns spun evenly and uniformly by the conventional spinning procedures.

Fig. 6-23. *The magnification shows how two thin yarns are used to bind a thicker, softer yarn to form a novelty yarn.*

Bouclé Yarn

Bouclé yarns are made by combining one or more thin, tightly spun yarns with a soft-spun, usually thicker, completely different yarn. The softer, slacker yarn will curl back on itself, producing a random pattern of large or small loops held in place by the thinner yarn or yarns (figure 6-24).

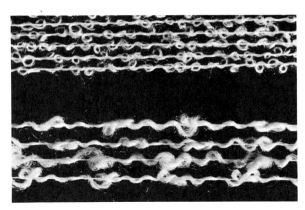

Fig. 6-24.
Bouclé yarns.

Loop Yarn

Loop yarns are a variation of bouclé yarns; here circular loops, all roughly the same size, appear at random intervals along the yarn. The loops can be set (heat-set) into the yarn or held in place by a folded-in "binder" yarn or yarns (figure 6-25).

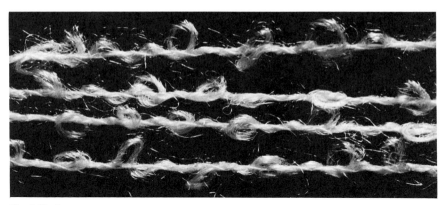

Fig. 6-25. *Loop yarn.*

Gimp Yarn

Gimp yarn is made of two singles and has a twisted or wavy core that has a thinner effect yarn wrapped round it to produce wavelike projections. Gimp yarn is a variation of bouclé yarn; the loops are not closed, are all roughly the same size, and are spaced in an undulating line on both sides of the securing yarn (figure 6-26).

Slub Yarn

Slub yarns have thick and thin places alternating along the length of the yarn.

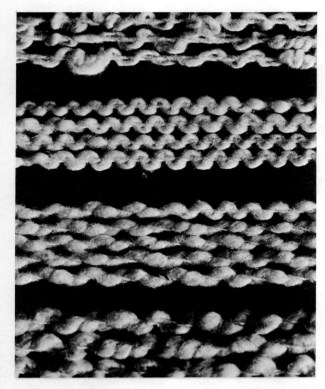

Fig. 6-26.
Gimp yarns.

"Spun" Slub Yarns Uneven spinning (generally considered a defect in ordinary yarns) is exaggerated to produce softly twisted yarns with sections in which the roving is hardly twisted at all. These "slubs" are usually inserted in fairly thick, soft singles but can also be produced by folding a fine, tightly spun singles with a softly and unevenly spun, thicker singles. This type of slub yarn will be stronger than the first type as the thinner yarn will hold the soft, unspun stretches of the slub singles in place (figure 6-27).

"Inserted" Slub Yarns Two foundation singles are folded together and have tufts of roving inserted at irregular intervals to form another type of slub yarn.

Slub yarns are popular because they give fabrics a linen look, since linen yarns have a characteristically slubby appearance.

Snarl Yarn
Very tightly twisted yarns will have small sections along the length twist back on themselves (figure 6-28). These snarls can be made to appear irregularly on their own or in groups of several snarls. The size of the snarls can be varied, and several yarns can be folded with conventional, uniform singles to make combined snarl yarns.

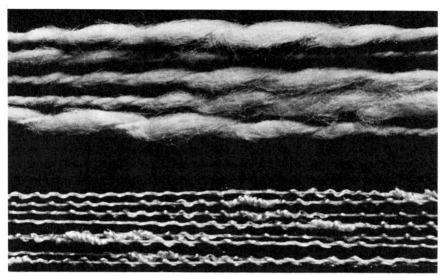

Fig. 6-27. *Slub yarns.*

Fig. 6-28. *Snarl yarn.*

Crêpe Yarn

Crêpe yarns were originally made of reeled silk filament. The silk filament singles, generally of 13/15 denier, were "thrown" (folded) in two pairs of S-twist and Z-twist yarns at 60 to 85 TPI, then cabled together in an S-twist at about 4 TPI. This procedure makes a very tightly twisted yarn. Fabrics made of it are reasonably wrinkle resistant and have a pebbly, crinkled surface.

Crêpe yarns can be made of any fiber. They are cabled yarns giving the characteristic crêpe look to fabrics made of them.

Chenille Yarn

By using a central core of folded hard-twist yarns, it is possible to anchor yarn pieces in such a way that they stick out all along the yarn length (figure 6-29).

Chenilles are also made by weaving fabric with warp threads arranged in small groups of two to six ends. This fabric is eventually cut into warp-way strips to make the chenille yarn.

Fig. 6-29. *Chenille yarn.*

Brushed Yarn

Yarns made of long staples, such as mohair or luster wools, can be "brushed" (teased out of the yarn structure) to give a fuzzy, soft look to yarns which otherwise may appear harsh and shiny. Long-stapled yarns are necessary so that enough of the staple will stay anchored in the yarn structure for it to remain sufficiently strong. Some brushed yarns are folded with tightly spun, thin yarns to form a tougher yarn structure (figure 6-30).

The best-known "brushed" yarns are made of mohair fiber, but brushing can be done on any sufficiently long-stapled fiber. The wrapper around the yarn package will state the percentage of each fiber component of the yarn.

Glitter Yarn

Metallic yarns are not often used on their own. Glitter yarns are generally a combination of metallic and rayon yarns, very often formed by coiling the metallic yarn around a rayon "core" yarn. Combinations of metallic with other fiber yarns are also available.

Fig. 6-30. *Brushed mohair and luster wool yarns. Note that the fine mohair has greater luster than the wool.*

7/ Understanding Yarn Thickness

Determining the width (thickness through) of a yarn poses a number of difficult problems. The cross section of the yarn is not usually circular, and, therefore, the often quoted yarn "diameter" really means the widest part of the cross section. For example, to test weaving yarns for the amount of yarn needed for a particular project, the yarn is wound, just touching, over a unit width. This procedure is described as EPI (ends per inch) or EPC (ends per centimeter).

Since we are not always talking about the diameter of a circle, it is difficult to work out the actual thickness, even though the length, volume, and relative density of the yarn may be given. An approximate thickness can be worked out by assuming a circular cross section. However, the TPI of the yarn or its component singles will affect the yarn thickness (figure 7-1).

A much more practical approach is to describe yarn in terms of a standard "hank" (a coil of yarn loosely wound into a skein), the number of folds, and the "count," that is, the number of standard hank lengths that make up a specified unit of weight. This system sounds very complicated at first, but putting it into practice is quite straightforward, and examples follow below.

Crafters who have only bought yarn in 1-ounce (25-gram) or 2-ounce (50-gram) balls or in other small packages may not be used to thinking in terms of yarn length. Different thicknesses of yarn are, of course, sold in different ball weights, so that crafters may tend to think in terms of the number of yarn balls they will need for a particular project rather than the weight of the yarn or the length of the yarn they will use (figure 7-2). A further difficulty is that stores categorize yarn into "fine," "sportsweight," "double knit," "worsted," and such classes. The yarns are also described by the ply number so that a 2-ply is considered a fine yarn, a 4-ply a medium yarn, and a "heavyweight" yarn that may range from a single to a 6-ply is generally just described as "bulky." These are very confusing terms for describing yarns, and crafters who wish to buy their raw materials in a more precise way need a far more accurate system to relate yarn thickness, weight, and length. Since yarns can be bought in bulk in the original, marked, yarn-mill package, and since the mills still predominantly spin their yarns to one or other of the traditional "count" systems (see table 7), it is very useful to have some understanding of these systems.

There are two types of count systems: the indirect system and the direct system. The yarn is counted in terms of stipulated hank, skein, cut, lea, or other lengths, and the *number* of these lengths to a given weight gives the yarn count in that system.

Fig. 7-1.
*Two 2-ply worsted 2.5s:
soft-spun on the left,
hard-spun on the right.*

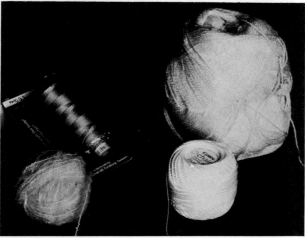

Fig. 7-2.
A variety of yarn balls.

Indirect Systems

The weaver or knitter who uses a great deal of yarn often buys yarn prepared for industrial use and wound on large yarn packages such as cones, cheeses (packages of cross-wound yarn on a cylindrical support), or cakes (unsupported cylindrical packages). These packages are marked with a code which may mean nothing to the layperson but which is readily deciphered once the meaning has been explained.

Imperial Counts

In countries with a long textile tradition, certain ways of describing yarns have evolved. A fixed length of yarn is cut from yarn spun from fibers prepared to specified standards. The yarn is counted in terms of the *number of hanks* of the particular length that is needed to make up a specified weight—usually the pound. The fixed length or cut varies with the fiber content of the yarn and sometimes with the region in which the yarn was spun, so that there may be several different counts for yarns spun on the same system. Woolen-spun yarn, for example, has several different count numbers to the pound as well as other count numbers that use a different fixed weight.

Two numbers are quoted for folded yarns. One number refers to the count, the other to the number of folds in the yarn. Generally, but unfortunately not always, the fold number precedes the count number. A 2/30s yarn, for instance, describes a two-fold yarn in which the two singles which make up the folded yarn *each* have a count of 30. The description must, of course, also have the count *system* specified, otherwise it has no useful meaning (see table 7). *Cabled* yarns are shown as two consecutive foldings (see sewing threads, below).

All this sounds very confusing at first, but it is quite readily understood after a little practice. The worsted count is used almost everywhere in the world, so it can serve as a good example for a detailed explanation. The worsted count is based on a cut of 560 yards to the pound weight. This means that a number 1 count (or a 1s worsted count yarn) is the stipulated length of 560 yards to the pound: one hank of 560 yards of this yarn weighs one pound. A 2s worsted count yarn means that *twice* the stipulated length, that is, two hanks of the yarn, will weigh one pound, so that 1,120 yards (560 × 2) of yarn will make up a pound in weight. A 50s worsted will be 28,000 yards (560 × 50) to the pound. It is important to realize that the *higher* the count number the *finer* the singles yarn. Because this is a back to front way of measuring in the usual sense, it is called an "indirect" system.

The count number refers to the singles yarn; a folded yarn is described by the fold and count numbers combined. This combination does not tell you anything about the *way* the yarn is folded or spun—that is another matter (figure 7-3). What it does tell you is that a 2/16s worsted is made up of two strands of 16s worsted yarn and therefore will weigh *twice as much* as a singles strand of worsted 16s. A 2/16s worsted yarn is roughly equivalent to an 8s worsted yarn, and this is called the "resultant" count of the yarn. In indirect systems the resultant is obtained by dividing the count number by the fold number. In our example the 2/16s yarn will measure roughly 4,480 yards (560 × 8; figure 7-4). This cannot be a precise measurement because the length will depend not only on the number of folds and the count number but also on the way the original singles were spun and the yarn was folded. A *tightly* spun yarn will be shorter than a *softly* spun yarn. Generally, a mill will spin the singles to be used for a particular type of yarn in the same way, but it may *combine* them in different ways. It is now easy to see why yarns from different mills may well differ in thickness. The mill may use an idiosyncratic count for the singles it intends to fold into, say, different sizes of knitting fingerings. Or the folding twist may differ from that of another mill. That is why Brand X may differ substantially from Brand Y even though both may be quite accurately described as "4-ply knitting fingerings." You can now understand why you cannot simply substitute Brand Y for Brand X in a pattern written for Brand X. It is not just a question of testing the tension; you also need to know how much more or less yarn you will need, and how it will react to your particular project (figure 7-5).

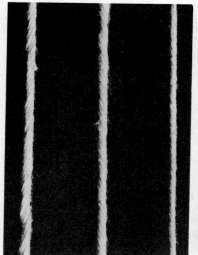 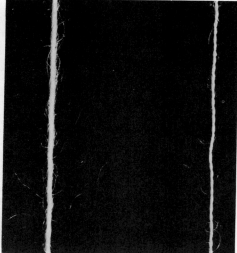

Fig. 7-3. *Relative thicknesses of 8/4s, 8/6s, and 8/8s cotton yarns.*

Fig. 7-4. *Relative thicknesses of a 2/6s and a 2/16s worsted yarn.*

Fig. 7-5. *A set of "homespun" 2-ply yarns; the yarn thicknesses vary considerably, depending on the color used and the amount of twist inserted.*

Metric System

The metric count uses a slightly different method from the imperial counts. Here a fixed length—1,000 meters—is said to have a number 1 count if it weighs 1 kilogram, whatever fiber or fibers the yarn is made of. The fold number is written *after* the count number so that a 15/3 yarn (often written 15/3 Nm or 15/3 m.c.) is made up of three singles whose individual 15,000-meter lengths weigh 1 kilogram. The resultant count in this case would be a metric 5 (or 5 Nm or 5 m.c.)—5,000 meters of this yarn would weigh approximately 1 kilogram. This is again an approximation, for the same reasons as given above.

Yarn Counts for Man-made Staple Yarns

As already mentioned in chapter 6, yarns made from staples derived from man-made filaments do not have particular counts reserved especially for them. Man-made staple yarns are spun in the way the mill considers most appropriate, and the count number used is the one usually applied to yarn traditionally spun in that way. A staple rayon yarn may, therefore, be spun to a cotton count, a staple acrylic yarn to a suitable woolen count, a staple polyester yarn to a worsted count. There is no set count for these fibers—they will merely "borrow" a natural fiber count or be described by the metric count.

Relating Counts to Knitting Yarns Given in Plies

It is useful to know how counts relate to plies of knitting yarns sold by ply number. Table 5 relates often used worsted or metric counts to ply numbers. These are the most common, although not the only, count systems used for knitting yarns and the table will give you an idea of how you can double fine yarns to make your own, thicker yarns.

Many yarn mills spin their singles to be used as plied knitting yarns to a 16s worsted or metric count. Yarns that are 1-ply, therefore, are often 16s, 2-ply are 8s, 3-ply are 5s, 4-ply are 4s, "double knittings" are 2s, and

Table 5. Knitting Yarn Plies Related to the Worsted or Metric Counts

	1 strand	2 strand	3 strands	4 strands	mixed strands	approximate resultant
2-ply	2/14 2/16	2/30 2/34	2/38 2/44		2/30 + 2/34 2/34 + 2/44	8s
3-ply	2/10 2/12	2/21 2/24	2/30 2/34	2/38 2/44	2/30 + 2/20 2/34 + 2/16	5s
4-ply	2/8 2/9	2/14 2/16	2/21 2/24	2/30 2/34	2 × 2/30 + 2/21 2 × 2/34 + 2/16	4s
Bulky (double knitting)	3/8 3/9	2/8 2/9	2/10 2/11	2/14 2/16	2/8 + 2/10 2 × 2/16 + 2/11	2s

"chunkies" are 1s, in the worsted or metric counts. You will notice there is not too much difference between these two counts (see table 7), and, for practical purposes, they can be used interchangeably, *provided* a test fabric is made before a project is begun.

High-bulk Yarns

High-bulk yarns are spun to a particular count for the singles in the usual way. However, the count is measured for the yarn *before* the high shrinkage potential singles are subjected to the hot water or dye bath which will cause the shrinkage. High-bulk yarns, therefore, are *shorter* than the length you would expect from the count number. One firm quotes its high-bulk 2/30s acrylics spun on the worsted system as actually relaxing to a 2/24s worsted count.

Industrial "Mill Ends" or "Lots"

Industrial mill-end yarns, that is, yarns left over from an industrial fabric manufacturing operation, are offered in a variety of qualities and counts. It is very difficult to find out which count system they were spun to, although the actual fold/count *number combination* is usually given inside the yarn package (figure 7-6). The supplier also often does not know which count was used. These mill-end yarns can be a very inexpensive way of purchasing excellent quality yarns; they can also be a trap for the unwary and inexperienced yarn buyer.

Fig. 7-6. *The label inside the cone gives the fold/count number combination but does not give any indication about the count system used.*

Woolen-spun Yarns

Many of the specialist wools are spun to a woolen count. As you can see from table 7, there are several of these counts in general use. Shetland yarns are generally spun to the Galashiels count, that is, a 300-yard cut to the fixed weight of 24 ounces. This works out to 200 yards to the pound, less than half the number of yards to the pound for the worsted count. That is why Shetland yarns, offered as 2-ply and 4-ply yarns, are said to knit to 4-ply and double knitting patterns respectively. They will knit to these patterns but will still be different from the ordinary knitting yarns used in the patterns.

Direct Systems

A direct system of measuring yarn was first established in the silk industry for reeled silk. The "spinnings" of several silkworms are reeled together to form the raw silk filament yarn. The unit of measurement, the denier, has already been described in chapter 4, and is equal to the weight in grams of 9,000 meters of filament yarn. The number of double filaments reeled together from several cocoons depends on the quality of the silk and the end purpose of the yarn. A common size is 14 denier. With the denier system of measurement, the *larger* the denier number, the *thicker* the yarn. This method of measurement is analogous to most methods of measuring and is called a "direct" system. The resultant is obtained by multiplying the count number by the fold number.

Man-made filaments are often expressed in terms of deniers. Both the individual filaments extruded from the spinneret and the tow may be measured in deniers. Tow cut to form staples will be spun into staple yarn and will then be expressed in terms of the system to which the staple is spun, as already discussed (figure 7-7).

Almost all filament yarns are twisted to some extent, because this protects the filaments from damage when they are being woven or knitted. The denier does not give any indication of the number of filaments in the yarn or whether it is a folded yarn, but occasionally the number of fils

Fig. 7-7. *The label inside the cone tells you that the original filaments were spun to 3 deniers, and that the yarn was spun to 2/20. The rest of the information relates to the "merge number," that is, the yarn batch and the dye.*

(threads) is given after the denier number. It should be noted that the amount of twist affects the denier and increases it substantially for yarns with a high twist.

Tex

A new, slightly simpler, and universal direct system has been devised called the "tex." This is an international system, which will eventually replace all other systems in use. The tex is the weight in grams of 1,000 meters of filament or yarn. The *higher* the tex number the *thicker* the yarn, making this also a direct system.

Information about yarn expressed in tex is given by an international code that works as follows: the resultant (R) tex (T) is followed by the fold number and, sometimes, the twist direction. As an example: R220T/2S means a yarn made up of two singles strands of 110 tex folded in the *S* direction, giving a resultant 220 tex yarn (see figure 9-11).

Relative Density (Weight Per Unit of Volume)

At first, the metric count, the denier, and the tex seem to solve the problem of different counts for different fibers—you might think that a cotton yarn having a 10/2 metric count is the same thickness as a staple nylon yarn having a 10/2 metric count.

Actually, you still must compare like with like. A wool fiber of exactly the same dimensions as an acrylic fiber will weigh relatively more—it has a greater relative density. So, if a particular thickness of wool yarn has the same length as the same thickness of acrylic yarn and both have been spun on the same woolen system, the two yarn lengths will have different relative weights. Acrylic "goes farther" than wool. It is, therefore, often sold in 20-gram or 40-gram balls instead of the more usual 25-gram or 50-gram balls used for wool to avoid confusion for the consumer (figure 7-8). The 20-gram ball of acrylic will be nearer in length to the 25-gram ball

Fig. 7-8. *Yarn balls sold in 20-gram or 25-gram weights, depending on the specific gravity of the fiber.*

Table 6. Specific Gravities of Common Fibers

Fiber	Specific Gravity	Fiber	Specific Gravity
Viscose	1.53	Camel hair	1.32
Cuprammonium	1.52	Mohair	1.32
Cotton	1.50	Acetate	1.30
Linen	1.50	Degummed silk	1.25
Dacron	1.38	Orlan	1.18
Raw silk	1.33	Acrilan	1.17
Wool	1.32	Nylon	1.14

of wool than to a 20-gram ball of wool of roughly the same thickness. Table 6 shows specific gravities of common fibers.

An important corollary of the different relative weights of fibers is the different relative weights of the same fiber type dyed with different dyestuffs. Some dyestuffs are "heavier" than others. Pastel shades may be produced by using one type of dyestuff, whereas deep shades may be produced by using another. It is, therefore, quite possible to buy precisely the same yarn but dyed to different colors and to find that the length and texture vary enough to make an appreciable difference in the amount of yarn needed for a project and in the way the fabric looks. The moral is clear: always make a test swatch of fabric.

Changing Systems

Although it is evident that some differences in yarns will not be pinpointed by the count/fold or fold/count number of the yarn, together with the count system used, it is nevertheless useful to find equivalents between systems. You may wish to compare, at least roughly, a Yorkshire woolenspun wool with a Galashiels-spun wool, say, or a yarn given in terms of tex with a worsted. Table 7 is arranged so that you need only locate the number 1 in a column and *multiply* the given count number by the appropriate "conversion factor" to change within a system, and *divide* the given count number into the conversion factor, to change from one system to the other. The conversion factors are along the *row* in which you found the number 1. Please remember that these figures are *approximate*. They do, however, give you a good basis of comparison for the different thicknesses in the many counts still used by the yarn mills. A small calculator is invaluable for doing the actual figuring. The following examples will make the methods of working equivalent count values easier to understand:

> *Example 1.* To find the metric equivalent to a 20s (British) cotton count, find the number 1 under the "Cotton: British" *column* heading. Read across the *row* to the "Metric" column heading, and find the conversion factor 1.69. Multiply 1.69 by 20, giving the answer 34 Nm approximately.

Table 7. Count Conversion Table

| Direct Systems | | | Indirect Systems | | | | | | | | |
| Denier | Tex | Spyndle | Woolen: American Run | Cotton: Continental | HANK Cotton: British Spun Silk | HANK Worsted | Metric | SNAP Woolen: West of England | LEA Linen Woolen: American Cut | SKEIN Woolen: Yorkshire | CUT Woolen: Galashiels |
9000 m/g	1000 m/g	14,400 yds./lb.	100 yds./oz.	1000 m/ .5kg	840 yds./lb.	560 yds./lb.	1000 m/kg	320 yds./lb.	300 yds./lb.	256 yds./lb.	300 yds./24 oz.
1	.11	.003	2790	4500	5315	7972	9000	13950	14882	17440	22320
9	1	.03	310	500	590.5	885.8	1000	1550	1654	1938	2480
310	34.45	1	9	14.5	17.4	25.7	29.02	45	48	56.25	71.98
2790	310	9	1	1.61	1.91	2.86	3.23	5	5.34	6.25	8
4500	500	14.5	.62	1	1.18	1.77	2	3.1	3.31	3.88	4.96
5315	590.5	17.14	.52	.85	1	1.5	1.69	2.62	2.8	3.28	4.2
7972	885.8	25.7	.35	.56	.67	1	1.13	1.75	1.87	2.19	2.8
9000	1000	29.02	.31	.5	.59	.89	1	1.55	1.65	1.94	2.48
13950	1550	45	.20	.32	.38	.57	.66	1	1.07	1.25	1.6
14886	1654	48	.19	.3	.36	.54	.6	.94	1	1.17	1.5
17442	1938	56.25	.16	.26	.3	.46	.52	.8	.85	1	1.28
22320	2480	71.98	.125	.2	.24	.36	.4	.63	.67	.78	1

Example 2. To express a 20s (British) cotton count in denier, again locate the number 1 in the appropriate column, read across the row to the "Denier" column, which gives the conversion factor 5315. Divide 5315 by 20, giving the answer 266 denier, approximately.

Crochet Yarns

Crochet yarns are marked with a number on the ball, cop, or spool package on which the yarn is wound (figure 7-9). This is called a "ticket" number. Crochet yarns are generally cotton and are spun on the cotton system; they are primarily cabled yarns produced in a 2/3 folding and ending with a Z-twist. Table 8 lists the ticket numbers and make-up of the crochet yarns produced by some well-known firms. It was not possible to obtain complete information on the make-up of all the yarns, but the companies DMC and WDC have given a breakdown of the way their crochet yarns are numbered, to what count they are spun, and how they are folded or cabled.

It is important to realize that similar crochet yarn ticket numbers from different manufacturers should not be taken as being identical in end result. A count equivalent is given in the table wherever the firms supplied

Fig. 7-9.
Ticket numbers of 3, 50, and 60 on various crochet-yarn balls.

it. The higher ticket numbers always denote the finer yarns, but a crochet-20, for example, does *not* necessarily mean it is twice as thick as a crochet-40.

Table 8. Examples of Crochet and Sewing Thread Ticket Numberings*

Crochet and Sewing Thread Tickets

Yarn	Firm	Quantity	Ticket Number	Metric Count	Cotton Count
Coats Mercer Crochet	Coats	20g	3		
Count equivalents			10		
not available		50g	20		
			40		
			60		
Cordonnet	DMC	20g	3	24/2/3	14/2/3
			5	32/2/3	19/2/3
			10	36/2/3	21/2/3
			15	40/2/3	23/2/3
			20	50/2/3	29/2/3
			30	60/2/3	35/2/3
			40	70/2/3	41/2/3
			50	80/2/3	47/2/3
			60	90/2/3	53/2/3
			70	100/2/3	59/2/3
			80	110/2/3	65/2/3
			100	130/2/3	77/2/3
Crochet Cotton	Mölnlycke	50g	3	3	
Resultant count			5	4	
only supplied			10	6	
			20	8	
			30	10	
			40	12	
			50	14	
Crochet Cotton	WDC	50g	5	4	
Resultant count			10	5.3	
only supplied			15	6.7	
			20	8.0	
Retors d'Alsace	DMC	5,000m	30	54/2	32/2
		10,000m	50	92/2	54/2

*Count number precedes fold number

Sewing Threads

Sewing threads made from spun staple fibers are folded or cabled to make very uniform, strong threads. Spools (or cops) of sewing threads also have ticket numbers on the thread support (figure 7-10). These ticket numbers refer to the thickness of the sewing thread and are *based* on one or another of the counts already discussed. However, the ticket number does *not* express the count of a thread in the same way. Different manufacturers ticket their sewing threads differently. Two examples are given below.

Fig. 7-10.
Ticket numbers of 30 and 50 on sewing-machine threads.

Coats Sewing Threads. Indirect System: British Cotton Count The ticket number in general use refers to *three times* the resultant cotton count of the thread. Therefore, a ticket number of 60 on a spool of Coats cotton sewing thread would imply a yarn with a *resultant* cotton count of 20. This does not give any information about the folding of the thread, which could have been folded in any of several ways. For example, the thread could be a 3/60s folded, a 2/40s folded, or a 2/3/120s cabled cotton yarn.

Gütermann. Direct System: Tex Count Gütermann Sew-All is marked with a ticket number of M303. The number 303 is decoded as follows. The last digit gives the fold number of the thread, showing it to be a three-fold yarn. The rest of the number refers to the decitex of the thread, showing it to have a decitex of 300, which is 30 tex (1 tex is equivalent to 10 decitex). The metric equivalent of 30 tex can be worked out by using table 7, as explained on page 106. The equivalent of 30 tex is 1,000/30 Nm, which is 100/3 Nm. Since ticket numbers are three times the resultant count, the M303 tex ticket number expressed in metric is 100.

8/ Making the Most of Yarn

The range of yarns in terms of color, texture, fiber quality and content, spinning systems, thickness, and availability is extensive. As each and every textile craft will be worked with yarn of some sort, the end product—the fabric—will very largely depend on the particular yarns chosen by the crafter. The method of fabric construction chosen affects both product and choice of yarn, for inevitably the crafter will exclude certain categories of yarn for a particular purpose. For example, fine laces can only be made with fine yarns, and any yarn with a tex count greater than 40, say, might well be considered unsuitable for a fine lace fabric (figure 8-1).

Fig. 8-1. *One-hundred-fifty-year-old, handmade lace.*

Although methods of crafting are altogether outside the scope of this book, it may nevertheless be helpful to discuss the type of yarn best suited to the better-known textile crafts. Provided the basic elements of yarn construction are understood, useful exceptions to the ordinary yarn recommendations can be pointed out, and suggestions made on how to create individual and original fabrics.

Fabric Design

Each piece of crafted fabric will have an end purpose. The crafter will usually decide before starting the project whether a fabric is intended for apparel, for soft furnishings, or for display as a work of art (figure 8-2). Sometimes several end uses will overlap. In all cases both the aesthetic and functional purposes of the fabric are best considered before the textile project is started. The look, pattern, quality, feel, drape, texture, strength, abrasion resistance, elasticity, and many other characteristics of the fabric will all ultimately depend on the properties and characteristics of the yarns chosen for the particular project (figures 8-3 and 8-4). A combination of craft techniques may also help to extend the use of any one particular yarn.

Fig. 8-2.
Imaginative use of yarns and fibers to create a work of art.

Fig. 8-3.
Detail of a tapestry weaving to show how yarn can be used almost like paint to create a picture.

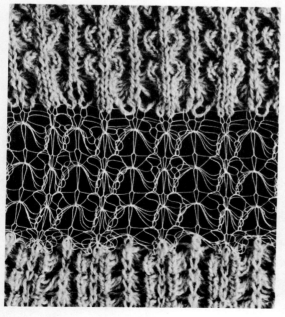

Fig. 8-4.
Two identical tuck lace patterns show that the choice of yarn has very considerable effects on the fabric made with the yarn. (Tuck lace is a type of machine-knitted lace.)

Differences between Weaving, Knitting, and Crochet Yarns

There are some distinct differences between the types of yarns that are useful for specific textile crafts such as weaving, knitting, and crochet, and the manufacturers supply very different yarns for these popular textile crafts (figure 8-5).

Fig. 8-5. *A soft-spun, superwash wool was used for this baby garment. A tightly spun weaving yarn would not have been suitable.*

Weaving

Although weaving is a craft with many different aspects there is one common denominator for all woven fabric, whether handwoven or machine woven, tapestry woven or braid woven, or woven by any other technique or combination of techniques. The yarns used for the weaving interlace with each other; the weft (horizontal yarn in a cloth) bends over and under the warp (longitudinal yarn in a cloth) in very different patterns but in essentially the same manner (figure 8-6). The fabric is a "two-element" one because *two* sets of yarns are used to make it. The *two* here does not refer to the number of different yarns used in a fabric, still less to the number of yarn ends used. The term *two-element* relates to the fact that two sets of yarns perform different functions. The warps form the basic structure of the fabric; the wefts weave in and out of this structure. The important consequence of all this is that the yarns remain relatively straight. Although the width of a woven fabric will be less than the length of the weft yarn used to form it, the difference in the measurements will not be significant. The weft yarns do need to bend around the warps, but only slightly, and, therefore, tightly spun yarns can readily be used. There is no problem with tightly spun singles creating a bias fabric because the cloth is, in any case, interlaced, so that it is "balanced" to some extent. It would seem, therefore, that any kind of yarn which is flexible enough to be called a yarn can be used for weaving.

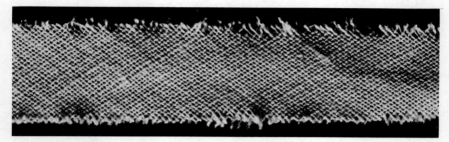

Fig. 8-6. *A cotton ribbon "yarn" showing the two-element structure of woven fabric.*

This is not the complete picture. The yarns used for weaving are, necessarily, divided into warps (also called ends or woof) and wefts (also called picks or filling). These two classes are quite distinct and serve different functions.

Warp Yarns The warps are the first yarns to be considered when deciding on weaving a particular fabric. These yarns will have to be beamed (wound on a roller) under a very high tension. This tension will be considerably increased during the actual weaving by the movements of the harness (frame used to lift or lower selected warps so that weft can be inserted), and, therefore, the yarns chosen for warp yarns need to be strong and elastic. Because the warp is rubbed by the constantly moving parts of the loom, the yarns also need to be abrasion resistant. If they are not, disentangled fibers will appear on the surface of the yarn structure, and the warps will cling to each other in such a way that it will be impossible, or at any rate very difficult, to insert the weft.

The strength of a yarn depends, to a certain extent, on its elasticity. If an elastic yarn is put under strain it will elongate before it breaks, and, therefore, its actual strength need not be as great as that of an inelastic yarn. Wool fiber is not very strong, but many wool yarns can be used with confidence as warps.

There are two reasonably simple tests for the strength and abrasion resistance needed in a warp yarn. To test strength, take roughly a yard length of the yarn to be tested between your two hands and stretch it until it is taut. Increase the pressure on the yarn by pulling your hands apart slowly and steadily. If the yarn breaks easily it is not suitable for warp. It is advisable to test several sections of a staple spun yarn so as to test the *average* strength of the yarn.

To test abrasion resistance, hold a few inches of the yarn taut between the thumb and fingers of one hand and rub along the length of this section with the thumbnail and first finger of the other hand. Do this a couple of dozen times, both backward and forward. If no loose fibers appear, the yarn is suitable as a warp yarn.

Fancy Yarns The way a yarn has been spun or folded will obviously affect its suitability as a warp yarn. Clearly yarns that are very hairy already, such as brushed yarns, or yarns with rather weak sections, such as some slubs, will not make satisfactory warps. Yarns folded with at least one strong singles can usually be used for warp (figure 8-7).

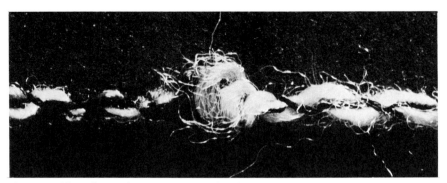

Fig. 8-7. *A "fancy" yarn that is strong enough to be used as a warp yarn.*

Weft Yarns The weft yarns do not have to withstand the same kind of tension or abrasion as the warps, but they do have to withstand beating-in (packing the weft against the already formed fabric). This means that very soft, fine yarns, such as some knitting yarns, are not suitable for use as weft because they tend to be beaten into virtually nothing more than a fiber pulp. Soft, *thick* yarns will be able to stand up to the beating-in, to a certain extent, and may be used intermittently to good effect. Even roving and sliver can be used for this purpose. Fancy yarns can all be used as weft.

Knitting
Domestic hand-knitting and machine-knitting are very different from weaving. Ordinary knitted fabric is "one-element" in the sense that only one yarn is needed to make it. This does not mean that knitting may not be carried out with several yarn ends at a time or that several different kinds of yarn may not be used while making a knitted fabric. It refers to the fact that such fabric is made by using one yarn (or several yarn ends) by wrapping (throwing) the yarn over a needle and interlocking this loop into the loops of the row before. No separate second yarn is needed for this process (figure 8-8).

Because knitting involves wrapping the yarn around a needle, knitting yarns need to be adequately soft and suitably flexible for this purpose. A row of knitted yarn pulled out of a fabric is very much longer than the fabric width—on the average, three times as long (figure 8-9). Therefore, the yarn

Fig. 8-8.
Stockinette-stitch fabric; the dark yarn shows how one row of knitting relates to the loops above and below it.

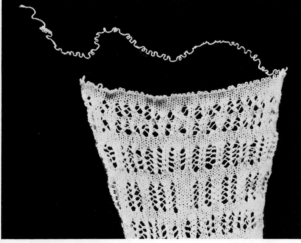

Fig. 8-9.
The length of yarn used for the knitted row is substantially longer than the width of the fabric; on the average, it is three times as long.

must not only be flexible enough to be thrown around a needle but must also be soft enough to maintain this structure after the needle has been removed.

Since knitted fabric is one-element, the twist of an "unbalanced" yarn will affect the fabric considerably. Singles, necessarily unbalanced, will therefore distort knitted fabric unless they are very softly spun, such as 1-ply "bulky" knitting yarns (figure 8-10).

The best yarns for smooth, uniform knitting are the knitting "fingerings." These are plied yarns that are medium- to soft-spun on the worsted system. Plied yarns are balanced and impart sufficient strength to softly spun singles to form a good knitted fabric.

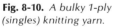
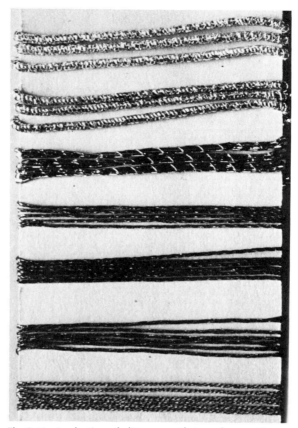

Fig. 8-10. *A bulky 1-ply (singles) knitting yarn.*

Fig. 8-11. *A selection of glitter yarns that can be used for knitting; such yarns, ending in a Z-twist, must be used with care.*

Hand-knitting Hand-knitting with the yarn held in the right hand and thrown counterclockwise around the needle adds a small amount of S-twist to the knitting yarn. As already discussed in chapter 7, the most suitable knitting yarns are plied ZS yarns. Hand-knitting thrown clockwise is better worked with SZ yarns. A skilled hand-knitter will not have any problems when knitting the Z-twist singles often offered as hand-knitting yarns. Lace knitting, however, where the yarn may be thrown several times round the needle to make large "overs" (lace spaces), is certainly more difficult to work if carried out with a yarn ending in a Z-twist. Many attractive glitter yarns end in a Z-twist and special care is needed when knitting lace with them (figure 8-11).

Machine-knitting Machine-knitting yarn is not "thrown" over the machine-knitting needles (figure 8-12). The yarn is simply laid over the needles or a set of selected needles, and hooked through the loops already

Fig. 8-12. *Fabric knitted on a knitting machine; only needles in the working position will knit stitches.*

on the needles to knit the row. The end twist of the yarn is, therefore, not as significant for machine-knitting as for hand-knitting, although a fairly tightly spun singles will distort the machine-knitted fabric in the same way that it does a hand-knitted one.

The main difference between yarns suitable for hand-knitting and machine-knitting is that the machine exerts a greater tension on the yarn. Very soft-spun yarns, such as some Shetlands or the Icelandic "rovings," are not suitable for machine-knitting.

Machine-knitting yarns need to be smooth enough to pass easily through various parts of the machine. Yarns that have not been specially prepared for machine-knitting can be waxed (passed over a block of wax or sprayed with a lubricant) to make them suitable for this craft.

Machine-knitting may be done with doubled yarns. Machine-knitters find it easy to use several fine yarn ends threaded through the tension assembly (yarn tensioning device). All kinds of yarn thicknesses can be built up in this way (see table 5). The machine-knitter is able to combine fine yarns to make original yarns of his or her own choosing. Hand-knitters *can* use this technique, but the needle may pierce such an open yarn structure and cause some problems with the knitting.

Doubling can be used to overcome the problem of machine-knitting with delicate yarns. Nylon monofilament yarns can be combined with almost any other yarn; this will add the necessary strength, but it will also make the knitted fabric much harsher and less flexible (see figure 5-11).

Crochet

Crochet forms a one-element fabric. Right-handed people generally throw a crochet yarn in the opposite direction to the way they throw a knitting yarn so that crochet tends to *unwind* an S-twist yarn and to *tighten* a Z-twist one. Although crochet is also made with loops, the loops are connected to each other one stitch at a time rather than one row at a time. Crochet yarns, therefore, do not have to be nearly as soft or flexible as knitting yarns (figure 8-13).

Fig. 8-13. *A simple crochet chain. Crochet fabric is interlooped one stitch at a time.*

Yarns specially prepared for crochet are generally cabled. The ZSZ cable twist is often used and so is the SSZ yarn construction. These yarns tend to be very round and smooth and not as flexible as knitting yarns. They do, however, make excellent lace-knitting yarns. Though cabled crochet yarns usually end in a Z-twist, they are so tightly spun that the small amount of unraveling which does occur in hand-knitting is not enough to separate the yarn folding.

Crochet fabric does not wear as well as knitted fabric and needs firmer yarns. Though most knitting yarns can be used for crochet, some do tend to be too soft-spun to make high-quality crocheted fabric; such yarns also tend to untwist during the crocheting, making it harder to work the craft. Some weaving yarns, on the other hand, make excellent crocheting yarns.

Knitweave

Many knitting machines have the facility to produce a fabric that is a mixture of knitting and weaving. This is a two-element fabric because a weft thread is woven *through* the stitches knitted on the same row (figure 8-14 and 8-15). The fabric is much more stable than knitted fabric, but it does not have the elasticity which is such a feature of knitted material. It does, however, extend the range of yarns which can be used for knitting, because the weaving yarn can be any type of yarn.

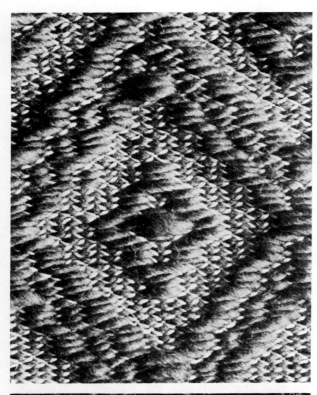

Fig. 8-14.
Knitwoven fabric: a bulky singles is woven into a knitted fabric base.

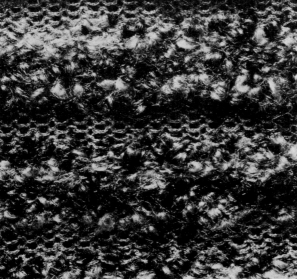

Fig. 8-15.
Bouclé yarns can be difficult to knit on ordinary knitting machines. Such yarns can be used for weaving into a knitweave fabric—the knitted base, worked in a weak metallic yarn, is strengthened by being doubled with invisible nylon (see also figure 5-11).

Working with Doubled Yarns

Industrial yarns (yarns manufactured especially for use on industrial weaving or knitting machines) are often spun to a finer count than yarns made specifically for crafters. This is because industrial looms and knitting machines are able to use very fine yarns, whereas much domestic machinery is not able to cope with such fine materials.

Finely spun industrial yarns can be combined in several ways to enable you to design your own yarn to some extent. Doubling the yarn, as suggested in table 5, is a simple way of combining fancy, plain, and textured yarns to make your own novelty, multicomponent, or colored yarns. For yarns wound on cones or other suitable supports, you can set one above another and slip the yarn from one package through the center of the support of another, unwinding the yarn ends together in this way (figure 8-16). The yarns will spiral round each other to form a softly folded, multicomponent yarn.

Machine-knitting suppliers and home-spinning suppliers sell small winders or spinning implements with which to ply your own yarn. The twist

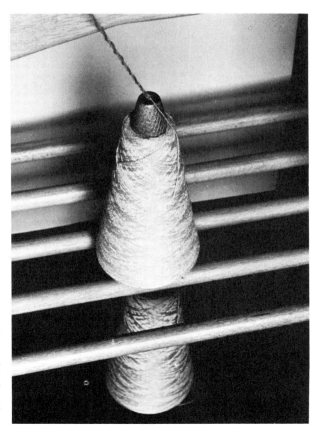

Fig. 8-16.
Yarn, threaded through the center of one cone placed above another, will then spiral to form a softly folded yarn.

will be more even and professional than that produced by the cone-over-cone yarn combination. You can also craft with as many yarn ends as you please, as already discussed.

The great advantage of combining yarns is that you can design your own colors and thicknesses and are no longer completely dependent on someone else's taste in yarn design. You can add subdued glitter to any yarn, for instance, or, for relatively small projects, you can even use a fine, strong cotton or linen core yarn and bind (wrap) it with the yarn of your choice.

Yarn Twist Direction as a Design Feature

The difference in S- and Z-twist yarns makes it possible to form subtle woven fabric patterns by using the twist direction of multifilament or worsted-spun yarn to reflect the light in different ways. The surfaces of warp and weft threads will touch each other in any woven fabric piece. Since the weft is woven (interlaced) over and under the warp, the top and bottom surfaces of the weft will touch the top and bottom surfaces of the warp according to the weaving pattern. Same-twist yarns will tend to combine with each other because the fibers all lie in the same direction. The fabric will tend to be dense.

When warp and weft yarns are twisted in opposite directions, the fibers will lie across each other, and will consequently be inclined to stay separated. Therefore, the individual yarns are emphasized in the fabric, and some weaving patterns will be made even more attractive.

As S- and Z-twist yarns will catch the light in different ways, it is possible to design fabric making use of this as a subtle design element. Such designs will produce patterns in light reflection.

Using Unraveled Yarn

Every knitter knows that it is easy to unravel a piece of knitted fabric; most knitters have had it happen accidentally at least once. Crocheted fabric is also easy to unravel.

Unraveled yarn is "reprocessed" yarn. At first this is hard to understand, but if you look at yarn that has been unraveled from a piece of knitted fabric (see figure 8-9), you will see that it has kinks in it from the knitting. Even if the yarn has only just been knitted you will find that it is definitely different from yarn which has not been knitted. If you are selling your work commercially—and this practice has only recently been permitted in the U.S. by a decision upheld by a Federal district judge in July 1982—you must understand that you may *not* sell work made from unraveled yarn unless you state that you used reprocessed yarn.

You may well not be concerned with selling your work. It is quite possible to use the yarn from unraveled knitted fabric many years after it has been knitted up. Carefully unpick the seams of the garment or other article. Find the place where the knitting was finished and undo the knot. Start unraveling the fabric pieces, one by one, slowly and steadily. You may want to wind the unraveled yarn onto a niddy noddy (a device to hold yarn in skein form) or a yarn skeiner, or you can simply make a yarn ball.

However, when you have finished unraveling the yarn, it is best to skein it and tie the skein in six to eight places. Soaking the yarn, in the normal cleaning solution you used for laundering the original fabric, will straighten out the kinks. You can make sure the yarn is completely clean by squeezing it gently in the water. Rinse the yarn, squeeze it dry, and hang it on a suitable rod. Slip a small weight onto the lower end of the skein (figure 8-17), allow the yarn to dry, and rewind the yarn into a ball or onto a cone (see figure 9-5). Your yarn is now ready for further crafting.

A good-quality yarn will stand up to this treatment. I have reused wool from a ten-year-old hand-knit sweater and have had excellent results for my new fabric.

Fig. 8-17.
A weight hung at the lower end of a skein of unraveled, cleaned yarn will make the yarn suitable for reuse.

Using the "Wrong" Yarn for a Textile Craft

Now that you know why certain yarn structures may not be ideal for a particular textile craft, you can mix and mingle all types of yarns to achieve interesting results. For example, tinsel threads do not make very good knitting yarns—they are too stiff and crush out of shape too easily. But they are still excellent yarns for some knitted fabrics. They can be knitted in with a soft knitting fingering or, more adventurously, they can be used in the "punch lace" pattern available on some knitting machines (figure 8-18). Here, the disadvantages of many tinsel yarns for knitting become an advantage. It is *useful* to have the tinsel relatively stiff, standing out above the basic knitting yarn, because the pattern gives a chain-mail effect which is rather attractive and certainly unusual. The disadvantages have been turned to advantage in the form of a particular design feature.

Fig. 8-18. *A punch lace (a type of machine-knitted lace) made with a soft knitting fingering and tinsel.*

You are now free to experiment, to manipulate and combine yarn as you choose. You have the knowledge not to use a yarn in the wrong setting and also to use a yarn, that ordinarily would not work in a particular textile craft, in such a way that it will work for you—for your original, creative purposes. Because you understand how to avoid mistakes, you can use yarn in many new and exciting ways.

9/ Buying the Best Yarn for the Least Money

There are several ways of buying the yarns you need, and each method has its own merits. Only you can decide which type of supplier will best meet your needs. Buying yarn sounds like an easy task, but it may actually take some time to work out the best sources of yarn supply. However, the effort involved in getting the right type of supplier, and then the right sources, is very worthwhile.

You have probably already noticed that there are no longer many yarn stores. Yarns can be bought from department stores and in some chain stores. Very often these outlets stock only their own brand of yarns or the best-known brand-name yarns, and then only the best-selling lines of these brand-name yarns. Of course, these yarns are very often excellent value—if not, they would scarcely remain competitive. However, if you wish to work with 100 percent natural fiber yarns or unusual yarns, you may find it hard to find the right supplier locally.

There *are* a few specialist yarn stores, and these can be delightful places to visit if you live close enough to one of them. Generally, specialists will stock a large selection of good yarns, including some of the more unusual yarns; alternatively, all the yarns may be special to the supplier and not available elsewhere. The proprietors of such yarn stores are often skilled crafters themselves and will be able to discuss your projects with you and perhaps offer some good advice about your choice of yarns.

Once you understand something of how yarns are put together, you may wish to buy your yarns straight "from the mill." Some yarn mills deal directly with the public, others will sell to people buying over a certain minimum quantity, still others will not sell to the public at all. You can find the names of mills that will sell their yarns retail by reading publications listing "factory outlet" sources. You do need to know enough about yarns to be able to buy without assistance from the people you buy from. If you want individual help, you must expect to pay for this in the higher prices you are charged when you buy from the ordinary retail outlets.

Mail Order

If you do not live in an area that is well served by yarn stores or other sources of yarn supply, or if you live a long way from any stores at all, buying yarns by mail order can be very satisfactory. In fact you may often be able to buy brand-name yarns cheaper by mail order than directly from a yarn store, simply because the suppliers' overheads may be lower.

125

Mail-order yarn buying is not for the impatient. If you like to buy on impulse, if you like to get the "feel" of a yarn before you buy, or if large yarn displays stimulate your creative ideas, you may not take to mail-order yarn buying. There are, however, advantages for the crafter who likes to plan and think ahead, and who can decide on what yarns to buy from examining a collection of small yarn samples.

No one supplier can be expected to stock all the yarns that are readily available nationwide or all the unusual yarn lines. The specialist supplier may only deal in linen yarns, say, or silk or homespun wool. However, if you study the list of addresses at the end of this book and add to it by reading suppliers' advertisements in the craft magazines, you will soon build up an invaluable store of places to buy your yarns.

Most mail-order yarn suppliers are keen to help customers buy the right yarns and are very happy to send you yarn sample cards for a modest fee. However, you should write and send a self-addressed stamped envelope (SASE) or telephone to find out how much the sample cards cost, whether yarns are sold in minimum quantities only, how long the supplier takes to supply the yarn, or how to place an order. Many suppliers refund the charge for their sample cards on the first order, but even if they do not, these cards are an excellent investment for you. You can build up an invaluable "library" of yarn sample books, swatches, and information sheets. Many suppliers also take great trouble to explain how their yarns are manufactured, and you can learn a good deal from their information leaflets. You can also make a comparative price chart (see page 135).

Once you have several sample cards, you will be able to choose yarn calmly and carefully in the comfort of your own home and with your craft books and patterns around you. It is true that color, in particular, is very deceptive when seen in a small yarn piece; the yarn color will always appear deeper when made up into a fairly dense fabric. But you will soon get the hang of it and will find yourself able to judge yarn color, yarn type, and yarn quality quite accurately even from small yarn samples (figures 9-1 and 9-2).

Fig. 9-1. *A selection of chenille yarns.*

Fig. 9-2. *A selection of bouclé yarns.*

Yarn "Lots"

Yarns are also sold at market stalls and craft exhibitions. You may be offered a selection of mill ends. These yarn lots can be a source of excellent yarn bargains, but there are one or two points you need to be aware of. The yarns are usually marked with a count/fold or a fold/count *number*, but they are not always marked with the *name* of the count. The number combination may not be enough to describe the yarn adequately. Even if the supplier is able to tell you that the yarn is a woolen one, say, you still do not know *which* woolen count it was spun to.

You can always buy some yarn and take it home with you to analyze for yourself before you do any crafting with it. The purpose of this book has been to show you how to use almost *any* yarn in some way for almost *any* textile craft. Provided you understand the difficulties that *can* arise, you may be able to circumvent them. You will be able to distinguish between a worsted- and a woolen-spun yarn, and you will be able to determine the folding simply by untwisting the yarn into its separate component strands. A magnifying glass will help if you have purchased a fancy yarn (figures 9-3 and 9-4). If you wish to find the count equivalent of the yarn, you can always unwind a specific length and weigh it—that is, you can establish an equivalent count for it. That way you will be able to determine how far the yarn will go for any particular textile project you have in mind.

A much more difficult problem that may arise is that a man-made fiber yarn may not have been put through the necessary heat-setting processes. Unwinding a small amount of yarn, stretching it taut, and then releasing it will give you an idea of the "relaxation factor" in the yarn. You can also subject the yarn or, better, a piece of test fabric made from the yarn, to the cleaning process you intend to use on the finished article. This will give you

Fig. 9-3. *Using a magnifying glass on a yarn can tell you a good deal about the yarn. This gimp yarn is made of softly spun cotton bound with a firm binder yarn.*

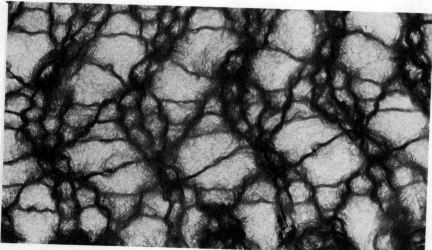

Fig. 9-4. *This mohair-type brushed yarn can be used very effectively for a knitted-lace fabric.*

an idea of the heat or moisture shrinkage of the yarn. You may find yourself having to do some preliminary work on an unbranded yarn, but you will be equipped to purchase unusual and inexpensive yarns.

Yarn Packages

Yarn can be bought wound on all kinds of packages (figures 9-5 and 9-6). At one time, yarn was sold in hanks or skeins (figure 9-7), and occasionally it still is, but most yarn now sold in the ordinary retail outlets is sold in yarn "balls" (figure 9-8) weighing between 20 and 100 grams. Yarns are sold wound into these relatively small quantities, so that each customer can buy approximately the amount of yarn needed for a particular project without having too much left over.

Fig. 9-5. *Left to right: a yarn ball wound on a yarn winder, a store yarn ball, a hand-wound ball, and a cone.*

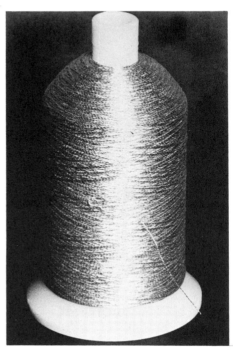

Fig. 9-6.
A bicone of metallic yarn.

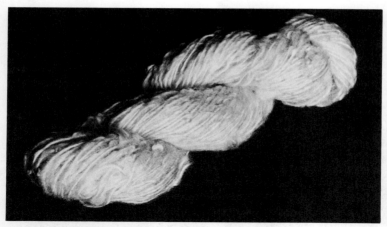

Fig. 9-7. *A skein of hand-spun Wensleydale.*

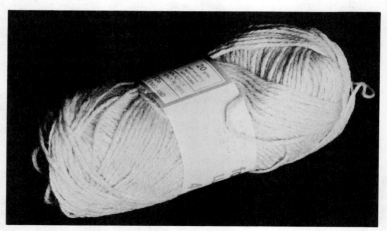

Fig. 9-8. *A common form of yarn ball.*

If yarn is bought from mail-order suppliers, yarn mills, specialist suppliers, weaving yarn suppliers, machine-knitting yarn suppliers, or yarns sold as mill ends, you may find the yarn wound on large cones, cops, or even cheeses (yarns crosswound on a cylindrical support). There may be 10 pounds or 5 kilograms of yarn on each package, but the yarn will be less expensive bought in this way. A further advantage is that there will (or should) be very few joins in the yarn.

The amount of yarn in a package may be too much for you, and you may wish to transfer yarn from a large package to a small ball or cone form. Ball and cone winders are available from weaving or machine-knitting suppliers (figure 9-9). Hank or skein winders are also available and simplify

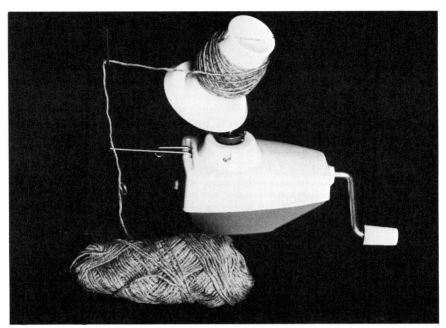

Fig. 9-9. *A yarn ball winder; the yarn here is being rewound from a yarn ball to make it suitable for fast machine-knitting.*

reskeining as well as unskeining yarn that is, say, to be unraveled or dyed. These aids can be used to rewind yarn into several small packages, so that you can work with several yarn ends of the same yarn or can share bulk-bought yarn with fellow crafters. Weavers will, of course, need the necessary equipment to wind yarns onto pirns (narrow cylindrical packages for weft yarns) or bobbins (small yarn packages that carry the weft yarn in the shuttle).

Yarn Storage

Yarn needs to be stored correctly, or it may be damaged. If you buy yarns in bulk, give some thought to proper storage. It will be obvious from earlier chapters that yarn is best kept in a dust-free environment and that light should be excluded if possible. I find loosely-fastened, black plastic bags are good for yarn storage, provided the temperature in the storeroom is reasonably constant. As moths can damage untreated wool, it is prudent to include a moth repellent in storage places where any wool or wool-blend yarns may be stored. Not all wools are mothproof.

The atmospheric moisture content and the temperature of the storeroom are important. Ideally, there should be as little temperature variation as possible to prevent condensation in the yarn pack. Mildew is best prevented by a reasonably *low* temperature, even if some fluctuations cannot be avoided. The best temperature and humidity conditions are in the range of 60 to 70 degrees Fahrenheit (15 to 25 degrees Centigrade) and 40 to 60 percent relative humidity.

Buying Yarn

Yarn is expensive and you may feel that you should buy only the amount you actually need for a particular project. This attitude is fine if you intend to hand-knit a single article, but even in that case I would urge you to buy at least one extra yarn ball. You will need to make a test piece for good results, and you cannot knit with unraveled yarn if you wish to match the rest of the fabric precisely (see chapter 8). You may also wish to retain some spare yarn for both practical and design purposes. For example, you may like to keep enough spare yarn to replace worn welts in a knitted garment, or for darning, or for blending small amounts of yarn with it for another article you might like to match with the first. Coordinating your crafted fabrics extends their usefulness considerably.

Dye lots vary even when the dyes are produced by the most modern methods. If you run out of yarn and have to buy a second dye lot, you will be able to spot joins in plain fabric. All this suggests that it is better to buy too much yarn rather than too little.

Advantages of Buying Yarn in Bulk

If you are going to consider buying yarn in bulk or, at any rate, in fairly large quantities, I suggest you buy the yarn in the most economical pack for your needs offered by the supplier. If you *do* have yarn left over, you can use it to test patterns, color combinations, or texture combinations, to attempt new crafting techniques, and to design your own multicomponent yarns. And, as stated above, properly stored, it will stay in good condition for a long time.

Estimating Yarn Needs

The quantity of yarn you will need for a particular project can be estimated if you know the dimensions of the fabric you intend to produce. Estimating methods will vary between the different textile crafts.

Weaving

To find the quantity of warp yarn needed for the planned fabric length, the number of warp ends to be used has to be multiplied by the length of each end—allowing for any necessary wastage. This amount is then *divided* by the fixed length of the system used, and further *divided* by the count number of an indirect system, or *multiplied* by the count number of a direct system, to obtain the weight of yarn needed.

Example 1: Indirect system: To find the weight of warp yarn needed for a piece of fabric 15 yards long and 30 inches wide, using a 2/20s worsted yarn with 12 EPI (ends per inch).

First express all lengths used in inches, so that 15 yards will be given by (15 ×
36) inches, and the 2/20s worsted will be [(560 + 36) × 10] inches long per
pound.

Using the formula given above, multiply the number of warp ends by the
length of each, and divide the result by the count and the fixed length:

$$\frac{(15 \times 36) \times 30 \times 12}{(560 \times 36) \times 10}$$

which gives the weight in pounds and this comes to .9375 pounds. Multiply by
16 to get the result in ounces, which works out to 15 ounces approximately.

Example 2: Direct system: To find the weight of warp yarn needed for a piece
of fabric 10 meters long and 115 centimeters wide, with 5 EPC (ends per
centimeter), using an 80 tex yarn.

First express all lengths used in centimeters, so that 10 meters will be given
by (10 × 100) centimeters, and the 80 tex yarn will weigh 80 grams per (1,000 ×
100) centimeters.

Using the formula given above, multiply the number of warp ends by the
length of each end and divide this by the fixed length; now multiply by the
count:

$$\frac{(10 \times 100) \times 115 \times 5 \times 80}{(1,000 \times 100)}$$

which gives the weight in grams and this comes to 460 grams.

If there are several different kinds of yarn measured by different count
systems, then the calculations for each warp yarn has to be made
separately.

The amount of yarn needed for the weft is calculated by precisely the
same methods: multiply the fabric length by the weft width by the picks per
unit length. Now use the yarn's count number and system to determine the
weight of yarn you will need.

Knitting

Estimating the amount of yarn needed for a knitted fabric is not as straightforward as estimating the amount of yarn needed for a woven one. One
reason is that knitted fabric is normally shaped while it is being knitted, so
there may be no simple way of giving the dimensions of the piece. However, even when the fabric is knitted by the yard or meter on a knitting
machine, yarn needs are not easily estimated. The tension or gauge to
which a knitted fabric is worked depends on the needle size or tension dial
number used, the stitch pattern, yarn, and particular knitting tension of
each particular knitter. If you unravel a single row of knitting, you can
measure the length of the yarn. This measurement is approximately three
times as long as the width of the knitted piece for stockinette stitch fabric,
knitted at the standard tension, obtained with the standard needle size
normally used with a standard knitting fingering. This measurement may
be quite different for a complicated stitch pattern, knitted in a novelty or

multicomponent yarn. You can make some guidelines once you have knitted many garments or other articles. It is very useful to weigh each section of a garment or article as you finish it; the weight will give you a good idea of how much yarn of a particular count and knitted at your chosen tension you will need to make such a piece in the future. For example, it is easy to estimate the amount of yarn you will need for a sweater with long, very wide sleeves and a short body-line if you have weighed and noted the weight of such pieces in the past. It does not matter if a short body-line was teamed with a short sleeve originally; what does matter is that each piece was knitted with a very similar yarn, in the same stitch pattern, to the same garment size, with the same needle size or tension dial number. The past information will then give you a firm basis for estimating the amount of yarn you will need for the new project.

It is also helpful to knit in a way which may be useful for making the yarn "stretch" to a full garment. If you knit the sleeves after you have completed the body sections of a sweater, for example, the length of the sleeve can be adjusted to the amount of yarn you still have left. Halve the remaining yarn, rewinding some onto another package if necessary, and knit the sleeve from the sleeve-head to the cuff. Knit until you have used almost half the yarn, then finish the sleeve with an appropriate welt. You will have enough yarn to finish the other sleeve in the same way.

Marking Yarn Packages
It may be useful to buy yarn in quite large quantities. You may well use only part of a large yarn package. It is very useful to mark the weight of the yarn left on the inside of the package. Remember to allow for the weight of any

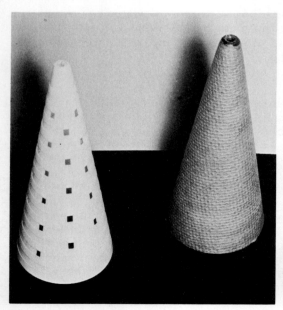

Fig. 9-10.
Two types of yarn support. The plastic support on the left weighs less than the cardboard support on the right.

yarn support; you will know what this is from the original order—yarn is usually sold by weight *excluding* the yarn support. Alternatively, weigh a similar support to find the amount you need to deduct (figure 9-10).

Yarn Is Sold by Weight

Some people may be confused by the fact that crafting with two or more ends of fine yarn will cost them more than crafting with one end. The yarn is sold by weight. The *amount* of yarn you use will depend on the technique you use, the size of the knitting needles, how you space your warps, or any of several other variables. Therefore, the *density* of the fabric will also be a factor: that is why one end of fine yarn "goes farther" than two or more ends used together. You may be paying more for your fabric because you are producing a "heavier" fabric, but the cost of the *yarn* does not vary.

Yarn Prices

The pricing structure of yarns is quite complicated. You will not be surprised to find that a high-quality silk is more expensive than a high quality viscose which resembles silk. However, the reasons for one yarn being more expensive than another may be more complicated than that. Among silk yarns, for example, one may be reeled silk and another spun silk. The method of spinning may also contribute to the cost of the yarn. All this is relatively elementary. The real problems come when the cost of the *same* yarn varies from one source to another. This may be because, as already stated, the supplier who charges a low price is simply selling yarn to someone he expects will know and understand these raw materials. No help is offered; yarn is simply sent or picked up in bulk quantities. The supplier has much lower overheads, another benefit passed on to the buyer.

Other savings can be made by knowing enough about yarn to recognize a brand-name yarn on a very large, unmarked yarn package, and then rewinding this yarn into smaller packages on your own equipment. In this way, top quality yarn can be bought and shared by a group of people at relatively little cost.

A good method for obtaining yarn very inexpensively is to buy "yarn lots." Many suppliers offer such yarns at substantial savings over prese-lected yarns and, provided you are prepared to accept substitute colors and thicknesses, you can often combine such yarns to make excellent raw materials for your crafts.

You will, of course, need to do a certain amount of preliminary work: analyzing the yarn in various ways, folding it, doubling it, and so on. The surprising thing is that you are often inspired to use yarns in unusual ways simply by having an unexpected selection of yarns available.

Comparative Price Chart

Yarns are sold in different counts, with different fiber contents, on different supports, in different packages, in different minimum weights, with or without postal charges, and so on. How do you compare one yarn price with another? It certainly is not easy.

One way is to make yourself a price chart for yarns of similar fiber content. Work out the price per unit of weight—ounce, pound, gram, 25-gram, kilogram, or whatever you decide. It may well depend on the quantities you generally buy yarn in. The gram is a useful unit because it is easy to compare the imperial and metric weights simply by remembering that one ounce is approximately 28 grams and that one pound is approximately 454 grams. If you list your prices in terms of the smallest unit, you can compare them very easily. If the amount of yarn you buy is likely to include postal charges, or traveling costs to a store or mill, it is only sensible to include such charges in the unit prices you work out for these yarns.

Price Comparison between Three Qualities of Shetland Wool
The following comparison will give you an indication of how to compare similar-sounding but actually quite different yarns.

(1) "Industrial" Shetland wool—this is actually a Shetland-type wool, spun to look like Shetland wool but made from the fleece of breeds other than Shetland sheep. Cost: $40 for 10-pound minimum weight, offered in a choice of five "named" (no samples) colors, and supplied "unscoured," that is with the spinning oil still in the wool. Marked R220T/2. Postage is included in the price (figure 9-11).

(2) "Real" Shetland wool from a specialist supplier in Lerwick (Shetland Isles). Cost: $9 for a 250-gram cone, available in a good range of colors that can be chosen from a sample card, and supplied "clean." Marked 2/18. Postage is not included in the price (figure 9-12).

(3) "Hand-spun, pure" Shetland wool, supplied by a cooperative based in the Shetland Isles. Cost: $2 for one ounce, available in a range of four natural (undyed) colors, supplied scoured and in hanks. Described as 2-ply, but with no indication of the thickness of the yarn except for the small samples sent out. Postage is not included in the price (figure 9-13).

First, compare the prices. There are postal charges for two of the qualities, so these have to be taken into account. The prices break down to the following, including postage where applicable: (1) costs $.0088 a gram, (2) will be $.038 a gram, and (3) will be $.74 a gram. In other words, (3) is very nearly twice as expensive as (2), and (2) is roughly four times as expensive as (1).

The price you choose to pay depends entirely on the end use to which

Fig. 9-11.
This industrial yarn is marked with a tex number and made in Scotland. It is not a true Shetland yarn.

Fig. 9-12.
*This yarn is marked
with a count/fold
combination that is ac-
tually a Galashiels
count, but this is not
stated. This is a true
Shetland yarn.*

Fig. 9-13.
*These yarns are
marked as true Shet-
land yarns on the sam-
ple card, but the size is
simply given as "2-ply."*

you wish to put the fabric. Your understanding of yarns will suggest to you
that the cheapest yarn in this range will not last as well as the more
expensive yarns. The hand-spun yarn is unlikely to give better *wear* than
the medium priced yarn, and you would only use it if you specially wanted
the homespun look.

The cheapest yarn will not be quite as cheap as it at first appeared: you
will be paying for the weight of the oil as well as the weight of the wool. The
most expensive yarn will be attractive to people who wish to produce a
fabric with a "hand-spun" look. The middle price will give you a good
choice of color in an excellent quality yarn.

The quality of wools varies enormously and is difficult to judge. Wool
quality depends, among other things, on the breed of sheep the wool
comes from, which part of the fleece it was taken from, the climate of the
area where the animal lives, the type of food and water available to the

animal, the stage of life at which it was shorn, the way the fiber was turned into yarn, and, finally but very importantly, on the skill with which the yarn was chosen for a particular purpose.

Home Spinning

A number of amateur home spinsters (spinners) now offer homespun yarn. Spinning good yarn is not a craft one picks up in a short time. You may be tempted to buy such yarn because the fiber content of so many industrially produced yarns is not 100 percent pure natural fiber, and you may also have the idea that homespun could well be better than mill-spun. This is not necessarily true.

Some of the larger yarn suppliers now sell homespun yarn. However, the word *homespun* does not necessarily mean yarn hand-spun at home by a modern spinster. It may mean yarn spun to *look* like the traditional yarns spun at home in the nineteenth century, but it may actually have been produced on a commercial scale by a large mill or on a smaller scale by a small mill that uses relatively old-fashioned spinning methods. The mills do, of course, have to compromise; their yarns have to serve many different functions. But commercially spun yarn is hard to beat for *spinning* quality. If you do purchase "real" homespun yarn, do get a sample first so that you can examine whether the spinning is up to the standard you have come to expect from the yarn mills.

Judging Yarn Quality

The quality of the yarn, that is how well it compares to others of its kind for the purposes *you* have in mind, is very important. Although a high price may be a guide to quality, it is not infallible. The salesman's pitch, "You get what you pay for," is by no means always strictly accurate. You will get the yarn you want if you search for it, and you will have to pay the market price for a particular quality. But if you shop around, you may find that the price you need to pay for the yarn quality you require may well be *less* than the price of yarn of a lower quality from a different source. It is true that a brand-name manufacturer has his reputation to guard, so that if you know nothing about yarns, you are better off buying his product than buying an unknown yarn at a market stall. You pay for the experience, reputation, and flair of a particular manufacturer, but the brand-name yarn price includes the cost of national, sometimes international, advertising.

Another way of buying the best yarn but for the least money is to learn to judge yarn for yourself by experimenting with different types of yarn, by studying yarns in stores, in mail-order catalogs, and at the mills. There will be times when excellent yarns from a new but unestablished source will be offered to you at discount prices, and there will be other times when you will be offered indifferent yarns from a reputable source. Armed with knowledge, you may well discover that one supplier's discount may still be more expensive than another's full price for an identical yarn. *You* have to be able to discriminate between categories of yarn if you wish to take advantage of good opportunities and pay less for your yarns, because it will be *you* who takes the responsibility for judging the yarn.

Glossary

Acetate fiber
Generic name for a group of regenerated, man-made fibers

Acrylic fiber
Generic name for a group of synthetic fibers

Alpaca
Hair fiber from the semidomestic alpaca or from the llama, both animals belonging to the camel family

Angora
Hair of the angora rabbit

Astrakhan
Yarn with exaggerated loops and imitating Astrakhan lamb fur

Bast fiber
Fiber from the stems of certain plants

Bave
The raw, double-filament silk fiber

Beaming
Winding warp yarn onto the warp beam

Beat (beating-in)
Pushing the weft yarn into place against the fell of the cloth

Binder yarn
A strong yarn used to keep weaker yarn components in place

Black wool
Any fleece color other than white

Bleach
To remove natural or applied color or impurities from yarn or fiber by chemical treatment

Blends
The combination of two or more different fibers in a yarn

Bright
Luster-reduced man-made fibers or yarns

Brin
Single filament of silk resulting from a degummed bave

Bobbin
A spool for winding the weft to be used in a shuttle

Botany wool
The term was originally applied to wool, tops, yarn, and fabrics made from the fleece of Merino sheep raised near Botany Bay, on the eastern coast of Australia

Bouclé
A French word used to describe a curly or looped yarn

Brushed yarn
A hairy-surfaced yarn produced by teasing some of the fibers out of the yarn structure

Bulked yarn
Yarn treated to form a yarn which is loftier and fluffier than the original yarn

Cable
To twist two or more folded yarns together

Cake
An unsupported cylindrical yarn package

Camel Hair
The underfleece of the Bactrian camel

Carding
Disentangling fibers and creating a web of evenly aligned fibers

Cashmere
The hair of the cashmere goat which lives in the Himalayan mountain regions

Cheese
A cylindrical package of yarn wound on a tube

Chenille
A novelty yarn with tufts inserted between binder yarns

Cheviot
A breed of sheep originally from the Cheviot Hills, and cheviots—singles used as warp yarns

Chlorofiber
A generic name for a group of synthetic fibers

Clean
Yarn which has been cleaned of industrial spinning oil

Combing
Parallelizing long fibers preparatory to worsted spinning

Cone
Yarn wound on a conical support

Cop
Yarn wound on a tube support

Cotton
The fiber from the seedpod of the cotton plant

Count
The method of describing the thickness of yarn by stating the mass per unit length, or the length per unit mass

Crêpe yarn
A tightly twisted, cabled yarn

Crimp
The waviness and spiraling along the length of a fiber

Crossbred
Any wool fiber, tops, or yarns below 60s grade

Cuprammonium
A type of rayon

Cut
A particular length of yarn; the length varies between countries and even between regions in the same country

Cuticle
The outer surface of the wool fiber

Degumming
The removal of the natural gum from silk fibers

Delaine Merino
A breed of Merino sheep

Denier
The unit of measurement for silk and synthetic filaments

Double knitting
Yarn that is double the thickness of the same mill's 4-ply yarn

Doubling
Putting two or more yarn ends together without inserting a twist

Drafting
Drawing out (attenuating) a prepared fiber mass before spinning

Drawn yarn
Yarn that has been stretched after being extruded

Dyeing
Changing the color of a fiber or yarn

Dyestuff
Material prepared for dyeing fiber, yarn, or fabric

Écru
The unbleached color of raw fibers, usually a light brown or beige

Effect yarn
A yarn which differs sufficiently from the main yarn used in a fabric to stand out as different

End
An individual warp yarn; or an individual single; also, ends—another name for the warp yarns

EPC
Ends per centimeter

EPI
Ends per inch

False twist
Heat-setting applied to thermoplastic yarn to cause it to bulk and stretch

Fancy yarn
Yarn deliberately produced with irregularities

Fell
The already formed part of the cloth in the loom

Felting
Interlocking of the scales on hair fibers

Fiber
The basic raw material of yarns, natural or man-made, whose length is much greater than its breadth

Filament
A single, continuous strand of fiber

Filling
Weft yarns

Fingering
Plied yarn especially spun for hand-knitting on the worsted principle

Flax
The fiber used to make linen

Fleece
The shorn covering of a sheep

Fold
To combine singles by twisting them together

Grade
The categories into which wool is graded

Grandrelle
A 2-ply yarn composed of two different colored singles

Grease wool
Unscoured wool

Greige
Gray goods; also, the color between gray and beige

Guanaco
The hair of a cameloid animal from South America

Hair
Animal fibers other than sheep's fleece or silk

Hand, handle
The touch or feel of a yarn or fabric

Hank
Yarn wound loosely into a package

Heather
Combination of colors in a yarn giving an impression of heather color

Hogget wool
First fleece from a sheep up to fourteen months old

Homespun yarn
Yarn resembling hand-spun yarn

Jacob sheep
Piebald breed of sheep

Jersey
A sweater; also, a knitted fabric worked in stockinette stitch

Kemp
The coarse fibers in the fleece of some sheep

Lamb's wool
Fleece from a sheep up to eight months old

Lea
The name of the linen yarn count

Line yarn
Fine linen yarn

Linen
Yarn spun from flax fiber

Linters
Whole or broken lint fibers removed when raw cotton is cleaned

Lock
A cut of wool from the fleece

Luster
The light reflection of a fiber

Melt
The viscous solution that is extruded through spinnerets to form man-made filaments

Mercerize
Treatment with caustic soda given to cotton and linen fibers to strengthen them and to increase their dye affinity

Merino wool
Wool from Merino sheep

Metallic yarn
Generic name for yarns which include metal in their structure

Mohair
Hair of the angora goat

Moorit
A tan-colored Shetland fleece

Natural fibers
Naturally occurring fibers from animal, vegetable, or mineral sources

Noil
Short fiber left after the combing process

Novelty yarns
Yarns with special spinning, folding, or textural effects

Nylon
Generic term for a group of synthetic fibers

Oiled wool
Unscoured wool

Pearl cotton
High-luster cotton yarn; also spelled perle and perlé

Pick
A single strand of weft yarn

Pilling
The accumulation of fuzzy, fiber balls on the surface of a fabric

Pirn
A small, cylindrical yarn package for use in a shuttle

Ply
The number of folds in a yarn

Plying
Twisting several singles to form a folded yarn

Polyester
Generic term for a group of synthetic fibers

Pulled wool
Wool from slaughtered sheep

Pure new wool
Wool marked in this way has to be made of new wool fiber that has not been used in an industrial process before

Rayon
Generic name for a group of regenerated man-made fibers

Reeling
Winding the silk from prepared cocoons

Reprocessed wool
Wool that has already been used in an industrial process

Reused wool
Wool reclaimed from woolen material used by the consumer

Rolag
A film or web of fibers which has been aligned by carding and then rolled

Roo
To pluck or comb wool from sheep which molt

Roving
A continuous length of fibers prepared for spinning

Scouring
Removing the spinning oil from yarn

Sericin
Silk gum

Sett
The number of warp ends and weft picks in a unit square of cloth

Setting
Conferring stability on yarn by heat treatments

Shed
The opening between the warps through which the weft is laid

Shetland wool
Wool from the fleece of Shetland sheep; also, wool from the fleece of sheep crossbred with Shetland sheep

Shoddy
Reused wool

Silk
The fibers spun by the caterpillar of the silk moth to protect itself in its cocoon

Singles
A single strand of yarn produced by spinning raw or prepared fiber

Skein
A loosely wound package of yarn

Sliver
A continuous rope of prepared fiber ready for spinning

Slub
A lump or bulge in a yarn

Spin
To turn prepared staple fibers into yarn by twisting them; also, to extrude melt through a spinneret

Spinneret
The gland from which the silkworm spins silk filaments; also, a perforated metallic cap through which a melt is extruded

Spool
A small, cylindrical yarn package

Spun silk
Yarn that is staple-spun from silk waste

Staple
The natural length of a lock of sheep's fleece; also, fiber of relatively short length

S-twist
The counterclockwise twist direction in which a yarn is spun

Swatch
A small sample of fabric

Swift
A skein holder

Teasel
A variety of plant with a bristled seed head

Teasing
Separating fibers; also, brushing fibers out of a yarn structure

Tex
International unit of measurement of the linear density of a yarn

Thermoplastic
Quality of being repeatedly deformable by applied heat and pressure without the use of chemical means

Top
A continuous roving made of combed fiber

Tow
The rope of filaments extruded from a spinneret; also, coarse or broken flax fibers

TPC
Turns per centimeter

TPI
Turns per inch

Tusser
Wild silk; also spelled tussah, tussor, and tussore

Twist
The action of spinning yarn; also, the direction of the spin

Warp
The longitudinal fixed yarns on a loom

Web
A sheet of prepared fiber

Weft
The crosswise yarns woven in and out of the warp

Wetting
Thoroughly soaking a fiber mass

Woof
Another name for weft

Wool
The fiber from the fleece of sheep

Woolen
Made of wool fiber; also, yarn spun on the woolen system

Worsted
Yarn spun on the worsted system; also, fabric made from yarn spun on the worsted system

Yarn
Any form of prepared fiber twisted into a continuous length

Yarn size
The thickness or count of the yarn

Z-twist
The clockwise twist direction in which a yarn is spun

Appendix

Mail-order Suppliers

This list includes only suppliers who sent test samples of their yarns and are willing to sell their yarns by mail order. I have indicated the supplier's *main* speciality (if it has one), but I cannot list all the yarns stocked. *Please send a self-addressed stamped envelope (SASE)* for information and shade cards, or *telephone* to find out the cost of yarn sample cards.

The following codes are for reference:
1: discounts available for bulk orders
2: minimum order required
3: postage extra
4: factory closeouts (mill ends)
5: weaving yarns
6: knitting yarns
7: crochet yarns

Bare Hill Studios & Fiber Loft
Route 111 (Post Office Building), Harvard, MA 01451, Telephone: (617) 456-8669

1,2,3,4,5,6,7 □ A large selection of brand-name yarns stocked. Specializes in all types of weaving yarns—wools, synthetics, silks, mohairs, cottons. Also stocks rug yarns and homespun yarns.

Beka Inc.
1648 Grand Avenue, St. Paul, MN 55105, Telephone: (612) 222-7005

3,4,5,6,7 □ Distributors for Perendale wool yarns from New Zealand, and for hand-carded, hand-spun, and hand-dyed yarns produced by the Quiche Indians in the mountains of Guatemala. A variety of mill ends and cotton warp yarns are also available.

B. Glumenthal & Company Inc.
P.O. Box 444, Carlstadt, NJ 07072

2,3,5,6,7 □ This company markets the "Lily" products. They offer an excellent range of crochet cottons in a wide choice of sizes and colors; also, weaving cottons, pearl cottons, embroidery cottons, and some rayon/cotton blend rug filler yarns.

Condon's Yarns
P.O. Box 129, Charlottetown, Prince Edward Island, Canada C1A 7K31

1,5,6,7 □ A selection of 100 percent wool yarns, some blended yarns, and natural-colored unspun 100 percent wool yarns.

Dyed in the Wool
252 West 37th Street, Suite 1800, New York, NY 10018, Telephone: (212) 563-6669

2,3,6   □   100 percent Australian Merino homespun wool, cultivated silk, wild silk, and a mohair/wool/nylon mixture. This company produces some of the most uniquely colored hand-knitting yarns available today. No two skeins are alike.

Frederick J. Fawcett Inc.
129 South Street, Boston, MA 02111, Telephone: (617) 542-2370

1,3,5,6,7   □   This firm specializes in linen yarns; both tow and line yarns are supplied in a variety of colors and counts. There is an outstanding selection of 2/20s and 3/12s weaving worsted, and a selection of macramé yarns.

Gemini Innovations Ltd
720 East Jericho Turnpike, Huntington Station, NY 17746, Telephone: (516) 549-5650

2,3, unusual 5,6,7   □   This company markets unusual yarn materials such as tubular satin ribbons; woven rayon ribbons; soft, bulky knitting tweeds and luxurious mohairs with a small amount of sparkle.

Glass House Fiber Imports
P.O. Box 105, Henwoods Hill Road, Westminster Station, VT 05159

3,5   □   This firm stocks a wide range of standard handweaving yarns, including woolens and worsteds, cottons and linens, rug yarns, and rug warps. Nonrepeatable items of specialist yarns, including silks, cashmere, camel, and so on are also available.

Glimakra Looms 'n Yarns Inc
P.O. Box 16157, Rocky River, OH 44116, Telephone: (216) 333-7595

3,5,6,7   □   An absolutely outstanding collection of linen, cotton, and pure wool yarns. The linen and cotton yarns are spun to fine counts (16/1 and 30/2 respectively), and the range of colors is quite extensive. These yarns can be used for bobbin lacemaking and rug making as well as handweaving, knitting, and crochet.

Heirloom
P. O. Box 239, 527 Avenue E, Rochelle, IL 61068, Telephone: (815) 562-4121

1,6   □   A good source of high-quality worsted yarns in 100 percent wool, 100 percent Orlon, and some blends. There is a good selection of colors in the different categories.

Kreinik Manufacturing Company
1351 Market Street, Parkersburg, WV 26101, Telephone: (304) 422-8900

1,3,5,6,7   □   Specialists in fine yarns, particularly silks and metallics, for all forms of needlework. Silks include *filament* as well as spun silk, which is very unusual, and both mulberry and wild silk yarns are carried. There is a full line of metallic yarns.

The Mannings
R. D. 2, East Berlin, PA 17316, Telephone: (800) 233-7166

1,3,5,6,7   □   A selection of specially skeined white warp or weft wool yarns in different sizes—ready for dyeing. This is primarily a handweaving school and supply center, but they also offer some unusual yarns for knitting and crochet.

The Niddy Noddy
416 Albany Post Road, Croton-on-Hudson, NY 10520

1,3,5,6,7   □   A huge range of all kinds of yarns, including specialty, novelty, hand-dyed, and high-quality yarns. Let them know your requirements, and they will send samples of interest to you.

Periwinkle
P.O. Box 426, Drexel Hill, PA 19026

1,3,5,7   □   Greek hand-spun wool in commercially dyed, plant-dyed, and natural colors; unspun wool in natural blends; Egyptian pearl cottons.

School Products Company Inc.
1201 Broadway, New York, NY 10001, Telephone: (212) 679-3516

1,2,3,5,6,7   □   55 percent cotton/45 percent linen blends for weaving or machine-knitting in twenty-eight colors; 100 percent cashmere; handspun/hand-dyed warp linens; weaving wools; good range of crochet cottons.

Settlement Farm
R. D. 1, Box 540, Cambridge, VT 05444, Telephone: (802) 899-2522

3,5,6,7   □   Homegrown wool sent to the Bartlettyarns Mill at Harmony, Maine. This is a century-old mill using early but excellent procedures for spinning the yarns. All the wool is spun into "2-ply" knitting and weaving yarns in sport, worsted, heavy, and bulky weights. Colors shown on sample card.

Straw into Gold
3006 San Pablo Avenue, Berkeley, CA 94618, Telephone: (415) 548-5241

1,3,5,6,7   □   An unusual collection of cultivated and wild silk yarns in natural shades, colored pure silk bouclé and plain yarns, space-dyed fine cottons and bulky chenilles, 100 percent New Zealand colored wool and natural rovings.

Tahki Imports Ltd.
92 Kennedy Street, Hackensack, NJ 07601

5,6,7   □   An extensive range of imported, 100 percent wool yarns, silk/wool mixtures from Europe, and 100 percent cotton ribbon yarn. A good selection of unusual yarns.

Three Bags Full Inc.
P. O. Box 455, Lexington, MA 02173

6 (can be used for 5 and 7); discounts by arrangement. A selection of unusual and beautiful hand-knitting yarn kits primarily supplied in natural fibers: alpaca, mohair, wool, cotton. Willing to supply yarns only if requested.

Underhill Yarns
1070 Barnegat Lane, Mantoloking, NJ 08738, Telephone: (201) 899-4353

3,6 □ Imported 100 percent Shetland wool yarn in "light" weight and "heavy" weight. A good selection of shades.

Wilde Yarns
3705 Main Street, Philadelphia, PA 19127, Telephone: (215) 482-8800
(215) 482-8800

2,3,5,6 □ A selection of 100 percent wool yarns, woolen-spun in a mill which has been producing fine quality yarns since 1880. The yarns are spun for the handweaver and the custom carpet industry, and the mill is developing a new line of softer yarns suitable for both hand-knitting and machine-knitting. Yarns are available in a good range of natural and dyed carded wools, berbers, natural white yarns in various weights, and a good selection of colored yarns in various weights.

YLI Corporation
742 Genevieve, Suite L, Solana Beach, CA 92075, Telephone: (714) 755-4818

3, unusual 5,6,7 □ YLI specializes in importing unique items for textile crafts. The range includes: an outstanding collection of metallics; silk, synthetic, and fancy ribbons; 100 percent silk embroidery threads; and soft sliver-and machine-spun silk in natural colors.

Yarn Manufacturers
This list covers yarn manufacturers who have sent samples of and/or information about their yarns and are willing to send you the names of sources of their yarns nearest to you on receipt of an SASE.

Bernat Yarn & Craft Corporation
Depot and Mendon Streets, Uxbridge, MA 01569

A really beautiful range of knitting yarns in all sizes, a very good color selection, and many "fancy" yarns. The range includes many 100 percent cotton yarns, as well as pure and blended synthetic yarns, glitter yarns, and some natural fiber/synthetic blends. Yarn pattern books are also available.

Brunswick Worsted Mills Inc.
P.O. Box 276, Pickens, SC 29671

A very good selection of high-quality knitting yarns in various weights and fiber blends. Also a good selection of rug yarns and needlepoint yarns.

Bucilla
150 Meadowland Parkway, Secaucus, NJ 07094

A very large range of knitting yarns, some in 100 percent wool, mostly blends of synthetic, or natural fiber/synthetic, yarns. Bucilla also supplies a good range of embroidery and tapestry, crochet, and glitter yarns. A selection of the "Filatures des 3 Suisses" yarns are also supplied.

Columbia-Minerva
P. O. Box 300, Rochelle, IL 61066, Telephone: (815) 562-4121

A good selection of knitting yarns in various blends and weights; also, crochet, embroidery, needlepoint, and tapestry yarns.

Fiesta Yarns
821 Canyon Road, Santa Fe, NM 87501, Telephone: (505) 983-5003

A small but unusual range of interesting yarns: 100 percent cotton bouclés, rayon chenille/rayon slub blends, cotton/wool/silk blends, and so on, all dyed with a unique, hand-dye process with no two skeins exactly alike.

Forté Fibers
P. O. Box 818, Palisade, CO 81526, Telephone: (303)464-7395

A small selection of unusual fiber yarns: 100 percent soft-spun singles in marble effects, lightweight and heavyweight one-color singles, 2-ply and 4-ply wools, alpaca, camel hair, and Persian cashmere yarns, as well as some fiber blends.

Grandor Industries Ltd.
P. O. Box 5831, 4031 Knobhill Drive, Sherman Oaks, CA 91403, Telephone: (213) 784-5855

Importers and distributors of British handweaving yarns. Yarns are especially prepared for the firm and include textured cottons, wool in the form of rovings and berber types, tusser silks, textured linens, and warp twines. The Sunbeam range of yarns is stocked for delivery from the California warehouse.

Lion Brand Yarn Company
1270 Broadway, New York, NY 10001, Telephone: (212) 736-7939

A selection of knitting yarns in 100 percent synthetics, 100 percent Woolmarked wools, blends, and rug yarns. Also a selection of imported yarns, including 100 percent angora. Lamé and glitter yarns.

Laines anny blatt
24770 Crestview Court, Farmington Hills, MI 48018, Telephone: (313) 474-2942

An inspiring selection of imported French yarns. Several 100 percent natural fiber yarns; blends including angora; some blends with synthetics. Also a selection of close-outs, knitting accessories, and design books.

Pingouin Corporation
P.O. Box 100, Highway 45, Jamestown, SC 29453

An impressive collection of French knitting and crochet yarns and acrylic tapestry yarns. The yarns are available in a large color range of plain and textured cottons, a large range of acrylic or acrylic blend yarns, 100 percent named and Woolmarked wools, mohair and alpaca/synthetic blends, and a good range of glitter yarns.

Plymouth Yarn Company Inc.
P. O. Box 28, Bristol, PA 19007, Telephone: (215) 788-0459

A selection of blended yarns in silk/cotton/polyester, wool/nylon, acrylic/wool/polyester, wool/rayon, and metallic yarns.

Susan Bates Yarn
Route 9A, Chester, CT 06412

This company markets a range of knitting, embroidery, and crochet yarns, and some of the famous "Patons" and "Jaeger" yarns from England. Patons "Fuzzy Wuzzy" (45 percent wool, 55 percent angora) yarns are included in the range.

Publications

The American Needlewoman
P.O. Box 6472, Fort Worth, TX 76115, Telephone: (800) 433-2231

Advertised as "your complete one-stop DMC shopping center in the USA." DMC markets an excellent range of embroidery threads, Persian tapestry wools, crochet and knitting cottons, and pearl cottons. This company also stocks some hand-knitting yarns and some rug yarns.

The American Wool Council
Wool Education Center, 200 Clayton Street, Denver, CO 80206

An excellent range of booklets giving information about wool fibers and yarns.

Lark Communications
50 College Street, Asheville, NC 28801

Three magazines in the group carry information on and advertisements for unusual yarns: *Fiberarts Magazine*, *Handmade Magazine*, and *Yarn Market News*. Although the last publication is aimed at retailers, there are articles of interest to the crafter on new products in the yarn market.

Needlepoint News
Box 668, Evanston, IL 60204

This publication includes excellent information on and advertisements for yarns normally used by embroiderers and needlepoint workers that may be of interest to other textile crafters.

Bibliography

Corbman, Bernard P. *Textiles: Fiber to Fabric.* 5th ed. New York: McGraw-Hill Book Company, 1975.

Davenport, Elsie G. *Your Handspinning.* Mountain View, MO: Select Books, 1981.

Hardingham, Martin. *The Fabric Catalog.* New York: Pocket Books, 1979.

Klapper, Marvin. *Textile Glossary.* New York: Fairchild Publications Inc., 1973.

Lorant, Tessa. *Yarns for the Knitter.* Wells, Somerset, U.K.: The Thorn Press, 1980.

Moncrieff, R. W. *Man-made Fibers.* 6th ed. New York: Halsted Press, 1975.

Taylor, Marjorie A. *Technology of Textile Properties: An Introduction.* London: Forbes Publications Ltd., 1972.

Teal, Peter. *Hand Woolcombing and Spinning.* New York: Sterling Publishing Company, 1979.

The Textile Terms and Definitions Committee. *Textile Terms and Definitions.* Edited by Carolyn Farnfield and P. J. Alvey. Manchester: The Textile Institute, 1975.

Index